The Warbirds of Walney

A concise and lavishly illustrated history of No.10 AGS

The Warbirds of Walney

A concise and lavishly illustrated history of No.10 AGS

By John Nixon

First Published in Great Britain 2014

Second Edition
ISBN: 978-0-9927514-5-6

This is the second edition of Warbirds of Walney.

We were fortunate with the first edition, to be allowed to include photos of the 60 Courses that passed through No.10 AGS thanks to kind permission from The National Archives, but we were restricted to a limited print run of just 199 copies, making the first edition a unique item. Due to public demand we have now produced this second edition which is identical in content to the first edition without the 60 course photos to allow unlimited distribution.

Graphic Design by Russell Holden
www.pixeltweakspublications.co.uk

Acknowledgements

Grateful thanks to Peter Yuile whose photo archive and extensive knowledge made this writing project possible. To Mike Gill and Barbara Huxley for their input of very personal family material and to all those who contributed their anecdotes and memories. Also as usual to my wife Philippa for her support through yet another project!

My thanks go also to my excellent typist Alison Smedley who continues to insist that my writing is "not that bad!", to Russell Holden my graphics wizard who exercises unfailing patience with me when faced with my most inane questions about computer technology and to Pete 'the pen' Langley for his cartoon illustrations.

To Ken Ellis (Fly Past magazine) for his input and support down the years, Gordon Leith (RAF Museum, Hendon) for his superb pictures of the collection's Boulton Paul Defiant. Tony Clarry and Gavin Conroy for the breath-taking photos of Anson K6183. Graham Pitchfork and Andy Thomas for allowing me to use their historic Defiant photographs.

Finally, my thanks to Pamela for all the delicious lemon drizzle cake. I follow your recipe to the letter but simply can't compete with the real thing!

For John and Joanne

The Author

John Nixon was born in Ulverston, South Lakes, in 1953 and attended High Newton Primary School. After leaving Cartmel Church of England School in 1968 he made his living in varied ways until he joined Her Majesty's Prison Service in 1974. After 32 years service, he is now retired and a self-employed writer. John is also the author of *"Oh Mother it's a Lovely Place"*, a history of RAF Millom and its mountain rescue activities, and *'Wings over Sands'* the history of RAF Cark & RAF Grange-over-Sands. He has enjoyed literary success in 2014 when the first edition of *Warbirds of Walney* was shortlisted in the Lakeland Book of the Year Awards.

Photo: Russell Holden

For more information about John and his books please see his website www.johnnixonauthor.co.uk

Introduction

As a very young boy it was Cark Airfield and its abandoned buildings and runways which first captured my imagination. They sparked a lifelong interest in the history of our nation's wartime air bases.

I suppose then, that it was somewhat ironic that my first Prison Service posting should be to HMP Gartree in Leicestershire; the site had been home to Royal Air Force Market Harborough during the war years (a heavy bomber conversion unit). Some of the airfield buildings and traces of runway were still to be seen, and I spent a great deal of my spare time poking around them.

In 1978, however, I transferred to HMP Haverigg in Cumbria. I was overjoyed to find myself working in what was, broadly speaking, an air base which had simply been enclosed by a fence. Over the 28 years I served there I slowly gained quite a fair knowledge of the site's history. I was also able to establish an annual reunion for veterans, many of whom became good friends.

In late 2009 I published my history of RAF Millom (No.2 Bombing and Gunnery School, No.2 Observer Advanced Flying Unit and their Mountain Rescue activities). In 2012 my second book, 'Wings over Sands', went into print. It was met with a gratifying amount of enthusiasm and the frequently asked question, "what about a book on Walney?" In response to this I began work on 'The Warbirds of Walney' in the early spring of 2013. Written with the aim of producing a concise, accessible and copiously illustrated history of No.10 AGS (Air Gunnery School), RAF Walney, which I hope will be of value as a work of reference to a broad readership.

None of this would have been possible, however, without the incredible knowledge and the large photo archive of Mr Peter Yuile, who committed both those and his time, selflessly and enthusiastically to the project.

Peter Yuile pictured with ex-Walney WAAFs
Mrs Marion Dyson & Mrs Elsie MacDonald 1987

CONTENTS

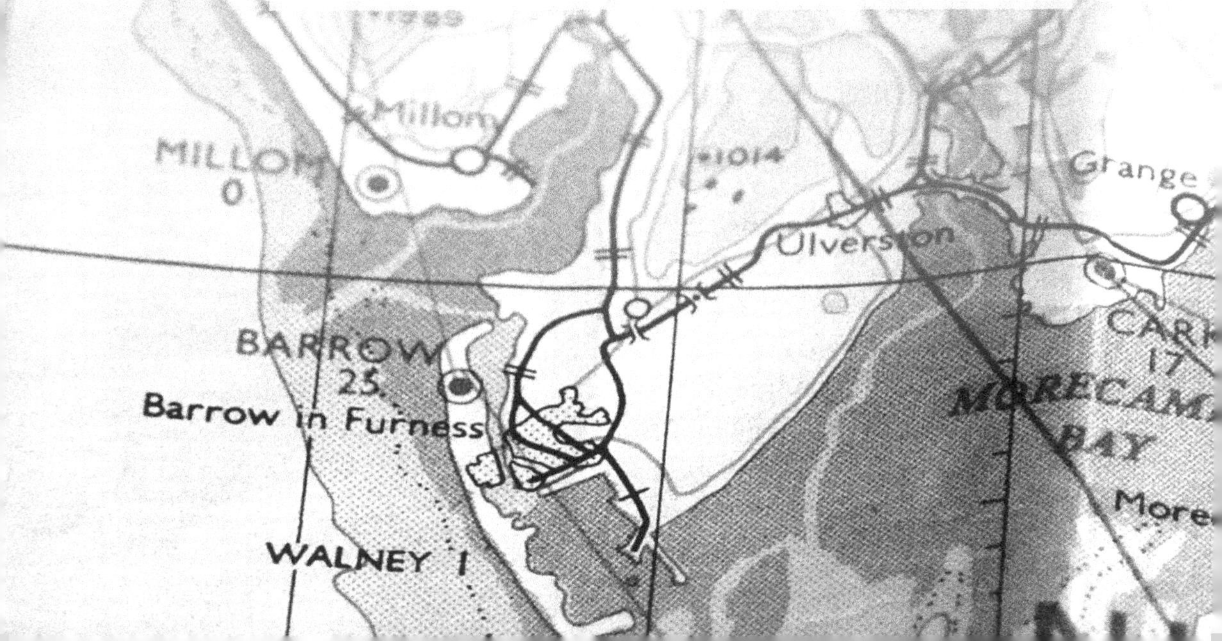

Millom
MILLOM
0
1014
Grange
Ulverston
BARROW
25
Barrow in Furness
CARK
17
MORECAMBE
BAY
WALNEY I

SECTION ONE

CHAPTER ONE

1941
Construction of RAF Walney begins

We can be certain that the construction of RAF Walney began during the first weeks of 1941. The exact date at which work on the airfield began is uncertain but the contract for construction was given to the firm Messrs John Laing & Son, who at the same time were building RAF Cark.

Coastal locations in which to establish Air Gunnery Schools were being sought by the RAF during this period of expansion. The main facet of an Air Gunner's training involved air to air firing at a target drogue towed behind another aircraft. The safest environment in which to carry this out would, of course, be over the sea.

RAF Walney was to be a large establishment with an average of some 1,500 personnel on site throughout its service life. The airfield's buildings were of a variety of designs, with the main site being over on the south east side of the station. Here were constructed a brick built control tower, three steel Callender Hamilton type hangers, several instructional buildings and the usual mix of offices and stores. Also adjacent to this site were two machine gun ranges. Over on the south side of the airfield were the dispersed living sites, with the Officers' and Sergeants' mess, gymnasium, education block, the Officers' and Sergeants' latrines and the station's sick quarters. Further south and close to North Scale were five living sites for airmen, two sites to accommodate the WAAF and an additional medical facility.

RAF Walney was to have a large resident staff. To accommodate them as well as the regular courses of cadets, 60 barrack huts, 66 Nissen huts, 18 Officers' huts and 17 huts for Sergeants were constructed on three additional dispersed locations. This would provide accommodation for 1,273 Airmen, 53 Corporals, 128 Sergeants, 88 Officers and 352 women of the WAAF, all in all a very large unit.

Target range at RAF Millom

It is of note that on two areas of the Walney site, evidence can be seen of two interesting elements of Air Gunnery training. On the western side of the airfield and just off the ends of the seaward runways are two gun ranges. On these two ranges cadets were taught to 'lead' a target using shotguns and 'clay pigeon' type objects. Mr Peter Yuile tells me that in 1943, whilst a young Air Cadet, he actually used this shotgun range and remembers that the shotgun cartridges were loaded with a tracer element to enable the trajectory of the charge to be seen.

Meanwhile, at the north end of the airfield and at the opposite end of one of the seaward runways, a moving target gunnery trainer and a rifle range are located. The moving target trainer involved a static aircraft gun turret on a chassis and a small gauge rail track. Upon this, a very basic wooden aircraft on a trolley travelled around the turret in a loop, giving the gunnery cadet experience in 'deflection' firing at a moving target. Both ends of this range were protected by concrete stop butts, understandably. One to stop and keep stray rounds from escaping, and one to protect the personnel operating the target trolley. This small target rail system was operated using electricity, though little evidence of that infrastructure can be seen today. The same must be said for the range itself as it appears to have been used as a refuse dump over the years.

Slightly to the north and close to the moving target range is a set of rifle butts - these are somewhat of a red herring! I can find no record of their use by the RAF, though I suspect that they may have made use of them in some way. These butts were actually constructed and used by the Territorial Army between the wars, though details are difficult to establish.

CHAPTER TWO

Autumn 1941
RAF Walney opens for business!

Whilst construction of RAF Walney began in early 1941, it was not until the 4th of October, 1941 that the site was deemed sufficiently complete to allow occupation by the RAF to commence. On that date an indent party, No.3 AGS, arrived on station. The party consisted of Flt/Lt Temple (Equipment Officer), 2 AC Equipment Assistants, 2 Sergeants and 2 AC Clerks.

It is clear that the conditions at RAF Walney were spartan in the early days of its occupation. On the 7th of October, the station's Operational Record Book records,

> *"Personnel 884(D) Squadron arrived on station, billeted on No.3 site and to use Sergeants' Mess for messing purposes and ablutions. As there are no cooks on strength, five ground Gunners have volunteered and will carry out the duties until the arrival of service cooks and butchers."*

From this date onwards, numbers of personnel on the station began to rise considerably, with Wing Commander C.J. Giles arriving on the 11th October, 1941 to assume command of the unit. On the 17th of October, four Westland Lysanders - the first aircraft to be posted in - arrived unexpectedly in foul weather conditions, followed on the19th by an additional two more. A further two more arrived on the 20th coinciding with the official opening of RAF Walney. Though their arrival is not recorded in the station logs, further aircraft had evidently arrived at RAF Walney as the records show that the station opened with twelve aircraft on strength: Ten Westland Lysanders and two Boulton Paul Defiants.

The purpose of RAF Walney was to train Air Gunners and Flight Engineers. This was a combined role for an Airman in the early days of the War. However, as Bomber Command began to receive the 'heavies' (like the Stirling and the Halifax) the role of Flight Engineer became more specific and specialised.

Throughout its service life, RAF Walney, like RAF Millom just across the Duddon Estuary, would provide a welcome haven for aircraft in distress. The first of these emergency landings occurred at 18.35hrs on the 25th of October, 1941 when a Spitfire from RAF Andreas in the Isle of Man made a forced landing at the unit. The landing must have been a heavy one as the station's ORB records that the next day a Miles Magister from RAF Andreas flew in with a replacement wheel for the aircraft. One day later on the 27th Sub/Lt Southern of the Fleet Air Arm, also force landed in a Fairey Swordfish after developing engine problems over the Irish Sea. There can have been nothing damaging about the malfunction as the aircraft took off later that day en route to RAF Millom.

On the 2nd of November, 1941 a meeting between the Station Commander, all Section Commanders and NCO's was convened. Under discussion was the moving of No.3 AGS to RAF Castle Kennedy, over the border in Scotland and bringing No.10 AGS, who were stationed there, to RAF Walney. The practicalities of such an exchange were explored and a decision was left as pending.

Whilst men and machinery continued to steadily arrive, it is clear that deficiencies were being felt. The 3rd of November saw Station Commander Giles and Senior Equipment Officer F/Lt Temple visit No.35 Maintenance Unit at Heywood to "hasten equipment demands for barrack stores." Also, on the same day, it is significant that Squadron Leader Bernard of No.10 AGS RAF Castle Kennedy paid the unit a visit, presumably to discuss the feasibility of the proposed school exchange.

RAF Walney 1942. Showing the airfield's 18 blister hangars.
Photo Peter Yuile

During November, work on the station continued and, whilst concerns remained the station's ORB states that by the 15th sufficient barrack equipment had arrived and been made available for 100 Officers, 140 Sergeants and 1,200 Aircraftmen and Corporals.

On the 25th of November and with the unit finally establishing some sort of routine, Wing Commander Giles was flown to RAF Castle Kennedy to discuss the finer points of the unit exchange between No.3 and No.10 AGS - the move was on! Officially,No.10 AGS arrived and were established as 'in post' on the 1st of December, 1941. However, as would be expected, in reality the exchange took several days. The unit was fully formed, up to strength and had been training at Castle Kennedy since August. As a result 47 pupils ofNo.6 Air Gunnery Course arrived from Castle Kennedy on the 5th of December 1941, followed byNo.5 Course on the 15th. Both courses almost seamlessly continued the training they had begun 'over the border'.

Courses would average around 40 pupils and these would be of all ranks from LAC to Sergeant and already qualified as fitters engine/airframes. Work would begin in the classroom with a great deal of theory and in the ground based turret trainer on the moving target range, the latter to prepare them for the next airborne phase of their training. This would involve being flown over the sea in the turret of a Boulton Paul Defiant, from which they would fire at targets on the sea and drogue targets towed behind a Westland Lysander.

The weather throughout December 1941 was very poor with winds frequently reaching 40mph and this was to curtail training to some small degree. In spite of the poor conditions on the 14th of the month, a Lysander, a Miles Master and five Defiants arrived on transfer from RAF Castle Kennedy – the unit was growing!

An early arrival at 10AGS was Defiant N1352 seen here whilst operational with 141 Squadron. Photo Andy Thomas

CHAPTER THREE

1942
The Unit Evolves

As the new year was ushered in, January was to be an eventful month, with No.7 Course of 24 pupils arriving to begin training on the 3rd. On the 8th and 9th the station was to experience the first three accidents involving aircraft of their own unit. On the 8th the station's ORB states, *"Accident to Defiant Aircraft T3989, Sgt Pilot Kowalczyk (uninjured), damage to aircraft not repairable at this unit."* The very next day we find the following entry, *"Accident to Defiant aircraft T4046, Sgt Pilot Hanzelka (uninjured), damage repairable at this unit"*. No details are given concerning these incidents, though records show that, at the time, the airfield was experiencing windy conditions with gusts of up to 45mph. This makes it extremely likely that these two mishaps were due to heavy landings. We cannot attribute strong winds, however, to the accident which occurred to Defiant V1173 on the 10th. The station's meteorological records tell us that the wind speeds were in the region of 10-15mph when the aircraft (piloted by Sgt Gaczol) came to grief upon landing. Doing damage to the Defiant described as 'slight' and repairable at unit.

We shall see as our history of No.10 AGS progresses that the accident rate involving Defiants was considerable, and frequently involved the aircrafts' undercarriage. With its single RR Merlin engine, substantial airframe and gun turret, the Defiant was a heavy beast and its approach speed on landing very high. The last surviving example of this aircraft can be seen in the RAF Museum at Hendon, and having examined its undercarriage at length, I personally was left with the impression that it does not look sufficiently robust for the task expected of it.

On the 21st of January, the airfield was brought to a virtual standstill by the arrival of 35mph winds and an incredible sixteen inches of snow! All available staff were mobilised and it is recorded by Wing Commander Giles that by the next day all runways and perimeter tracks were cleared and ready for flying to commence.

February, 1942 began as it was to continue with wind, rain, sleet and fog throughout. It is of no surprise then that little of note is recorded for the month. The exception being an exercise in airfield defence, which took place on the 8th between station personnel and Barrow-in-Furness Home Guard - No.10 AGS emerged as victors!

The 1st of March brought rather better weather conditions, though these were not to prevail for long. On that day the station's ORB also records that... *"P/O Menkes arrived from RAF Millom in Avro Anson 4900 at 11.00hrs, returned to RAF Millom 13.40hrs."* The purpose of this visit is unspecified, however, I do know something of P/O Menkes as he is mentioned in my book "Oh Mother, it's a Lovely Place", a history of RAF Millom.

I discovered during my research that Menkes was an enthusiastic flyer. He

Plt/Sgt Menkes (middle foreground) Photo Mr Bill Gracie

missed no opportunity to take low flying right down to the deck in order to scare the pupils and instructors on board his aircraft half to death. My good friend Bill Gracie, who was a Wireless Operator on staff at RAF Millom, flew with him regularly and remembered him well. Bill told me that Menkes chief ambition was to join a Mosquito Squadron. He was in fact granted his wish and posted to one from RAF Millom, but not before extracting a promise that Bill would try and follow him as his Wireless Operator.

Bill did not and it was his salvation, as only a couple of months after his posting word arrived through the grapevine that Menkes had been killed. What brought about his demise is unclear, it may have been enemy action (and probably was), or it may have been the type of behaviour which led to the coining of this phrase, "There are old pilots and there are bold pilots, but there are no old bold pilots!"

By the 3rd of March, the Walney weather was back in control once more with gale force winds, rain and thick fog forcing the cancellation of all flying. This was to continue almost unabated until the 5th of the month, when conditions began to show a marked improvement and flying was able to recommence.

It was to be on the 8th of March, 1942 that No.10 AGS was to experience its first tragedy. At 14.35hrs, whilst on a gunnery exercise, some three miles south of the station, Defiant N1811 suddenly stalled and dived into the ground bringing down telephone lines and crashing in Carr Lane, half way between Ocean Road and Biggar village, Walney Island. The pilot of N1811, Kpl Krol (Polish Forces) and gunnery pupil Sgt Lambert both lost their lives as a result. Kpl Krol is buried in Barrow-in-Furness Cemetery.

Yet another crash involving a Defiant occurred on the 17th of the month, though fortunately without fatal consequences. At 14.05hrs on returning from a gunnery exercise, Defiant N1742 crashed upon landing causing extensive damage to the aircraft, but leaving pilot and pupil unharmed. The cause of the accident is unrecorded and no specific details of damage given. It is clear, however, that N1742 would be missed from operational strength, as station ORB's show that four days later Defiant N3387 was flown in from RAF Brize Norton as a replacement.

To attempt to land a stricken aircraft on the surface of the sea, or to 'ditch' as it was known by aircrew, was to undertake a very imprecise and hazardous feat which, when carried out by even the most skilled pilot, could result in mishap. On the 13th of April, 1942 Lysander W6940 became lost in very bad visibility, was blown off course and out to sea. Faced with a strong north-easterly wind and on the verge of running out of fuel, the pilot, P/O Trilsbanch, and his crewman, LAC Bell, were forced to ditch their aircraft. Everything was against a successful outcome, the two main factors being the

rough sea conditions and the large cowling covering the Lysander's Bristol Mercury radial engine, which could potentially present as a 'water scoop' and throw the machine onto its back. It is testimony then to P/O Trilsbanch's skill and good fortune that the procedure was a success and both men were able to take to their emergency dinghy, to be rescued some time later. It did mean, however, that RAF Walney had lost yet another aircraft from its operational strength. Whilst all this drama was being played out, Course No.14 was nearing completion and all 37 pupils passed out as competent on the 17th of April.

Entries in RAF Walney's ORB for the 1st of May give a fair indication of the still incomplete site; the entry is as follows and was recorded by the station's Medical Officer, *"Sick Quarters are of a temporary nature and are situated in an Officers' barracks hut. Conditions are difficult owing to lack of water supply etc. In spite of the difficult weather conditions throughout the winter the general health of the station is comparatively good. A large number of cases of respiratory conditions ie Bronchial Catarrh and Nasopharyngitus, were treated due to the dusty conditions of huts etc before linoleum was finally laid on the bare concrete floors."*

On the 5th of May, at 01.15hrs, an Avro Anson carrying out a training flight from RAF Wigton struck a barrage balloon cable adjacent to the shipyards. It crashed on to Roosecote Sands from an estimated 2,500 feet and at a dive angle of an estimated 45-50 degrees killing all crewmen on board. They were F/Sgt Pilot E.Daniels, Sgt W.J.Perkins, Sgt K.J.Neill and Sgt H.V. Osbourne. The crash was a dreadful one and formed a timely reminder, if one were needed, that Barrow's balloons were to be given a wide berth.

As flying at the station increased with the settled weather of the early summer months, it would be reasonable to expect an increase, to some degree, in incidents and accidents. In reality the increase was exponential, with the Boulton Paul Defiant proving to be the unit's main protagonist.

It is fair to say that May, 1942 was a troubled and worrying month for RAF Walney, having no less than seven crashes involving Defiants. The first two of these occurred on the 15th when at 11.15hrs Defiant T3919, piloted by F/Lt H.N. Gravenor, made a crash landing on the airfield; no details are recorded. Only two hours later Defiant N1582 also made a crash landing on the station's runway, though for the first time and significantly, an undercarriage problem is mentioned. It appears that the aircraft's undercarriage refused to deploy, forcing its pilot (name not recorded) to carry out a 'belly landing' - it would not be the last.

Four days later on the 19th of May, an undercarriage problem manifested itself once more for the crew of Defiant N1700. Sgt Pilot H.T. Hatchard was in the cockpit with LAC Hilyer (trainee gunner) in the turret. The N1700 was building speed for take-off when the undercarriage collapsed, sending the machine in an uncontrolled slide down the runway and off on to the grass where it came to rest, fortunately leaving its crew unharmed.

On the very same day at 15.10hrs word was received from the constabulary that Defiant T4046 was recumbent in a meadow, some two miles south of Ulverston, close to the village of Great Urswick. The aircraft had suffered a total engine failure, but due to the nerve and skill of her pilot, P/O R.W. Somenson, he and his pupil gunner, Cpl Scott, escaped with little injury. As the day drew to a close the unit could have been forgiven for believing that things could not get any worse and that the day's mishaps were behind them – sadly not!

During the afternoon that same day, W/O J.Parrot had flown in from RAF Millom (for unspecified reasons) in a de Havilland Gipsy Moth, with Cpl G. Rose as his passenger. At 19.15hrs whilst gathering take-off speed to return to RAF Millom, the Moth suffered an engine failure leading to the machine digging its nose in and coming to rest upside down on the runway. RAF Walney's Medical Officer was to record that the two airmen escaped with "minor cuts and lacerations", a very fortunate outcome indeed, though it was more unwelcome drama with which to crown a very bleak day.

DH Gipsy Moth

From the 20th of May, the weather gave problems to flying training with very unsettled weather and intermittent thundery showers. By the 23rd the station was experiencing a strong southerly gale with winds in excess of 50mph and all flying cancelled. Overnight, the situation became much improved and flying recommenced.

This was to bring yet another accident involving one of the unit's Defiants when at 11.15hrs Sgt Pilot R. Jones crashed on the station's runway. No aircraft number or reason for the crash is recorded, though the station Medical Officer's report states that the pilot and his pupil gunner, Sgt O'Dowd, were unharmed.

May 1942 was to close with the loss of yet two further Defiant aircraft. On the 27th, Sgt Pilot D. Ravenhill, and trainee gunner Sgt Rogerson, made a forced landing in Defiant N3502 near Squires Gate, Fleetwood, following an engine failure. Though the damage to the aircraft was extensive, the two men escaped with cuts and bruises. Following what must have been an engine problem on the 30th, Defiant T4039 crash landed on the sand dunes on the north side of Walney Island. No crew names or an official cause of the crash are recorded in the unit's ORB.

With the coming of June, the station was sweltering under clear blue skies and enjoying very high temperatures indeed. Even this was to cause poor old RAF Walney problems as the tar began to melt on the runways to such a degree that they became unusable. By the 5th it was clear that some action must be urgently taken. Following discussions on possible remedies to the problem, it was decided to add some sort of additional surfacing to the runways as soon as possible. The next day, 100 members of station personnel were mobilised to throw 160 tons of stone chippings over the three runways to make them suitable for flying once more.

One of the problems experienced during this very warm period was that the Defiant pilots were finding their undercarriage units reluctant to deploy. The tar coated tyres were becoming 'glued' into the wheel wells! An undercarriage problem was once again the cause of an accident to Defiant N1637 when its starboard undercarriage unit did not fully lock into position which resulted in a crash upon landing. No injuries to F/Lt J.N.F. Hansen or his pupil Cpl C. Baldwin are recorded.

On a more positive note, training at the close of June, was progressing well with a regular intake of courses. Also, 40 pupils and 2 Officers of No.20 Flight Engineer/Air Gunner passed out successfully and went on to their respective postings.

With many floor surfaces yet to be covered by linoleum and with warm, dry conditions prevailing, the station's Medical Officer was still recording concerns over the number of respiratory complaints he was presented with. He was also monitoring the quality of food entering the station's kitchen, condemning fifty pounds of meat as "unfit for human consumption."

The entry for the 4th of July, also by the Medical Officer, states that he had visited the kitchen stores and condemned seventy pounds of brawn as unfit for human consumption. The quality and safety of the unit's food was clearly becoming a cause for real concern.

Previously, on the 1st of July, 1941 undercarriage related issues had begun to strike the unit once more. RAF Walney's Medical Officer records, "At approximately 12.15hrs Defiant aircraft N1744 (No.53) force landed on aerodrome with undercarriage retracted due to engine failure. Pilot was partially blinded by Glycol. This must have been ejected as a fine spray or as a vapour as there was little sign of the liquid on face or clothing. Rapid recovery after treatment by Sgt Pilot Evans and LAC Allen, no serious injuries." The Defiant's undercarriage was now obviously emerging as its 'Achilles heel'. Again, on the 5th and 17th of the month, N1636 and N1733 both crashed upon landing and both with undercarriage failures.

To add to all this drama, the alarm was sounded at 20.30hrs on the 19th of July. German raiders were reported over Liverpool and Barrow's balloon barrage was deployed at 2,500 feet. The alarm proved to be false with no enemy aircraft appearing in the Furness area, however, July and August of 1942, did see a rise in sightings of lone German aircraft. It is likely that these would be flying from bases on mainland France and quite possibly seeking 'targets of opportunity.'

It is surely an indication of the RAF's urgent need for aircrew that pupils were being posted to RAF Walney for training without adequate medical screening. On examination by the station Medical Officer, two out of ten (20%) were deemed unfit for various reasons. Representations were made and from this time on the station Medical Officer seems to have carried out mandatory screening.

The 29th of July closed the month in dreadful fashion with a fatal crash on the station's runway involving Defiant N1612. After attempting a take-off with the propeller in coarse pitch the aircraft crashed, rolling onto its back in the verge of the airfield. Sgt Pilot Elliott (RAAF) was killed instantly. The pupil gunner, LAC S Cooper, was discovered dreadfully injured but alive in his turret which had been thrown some thirty feet away from the aircraft by the impact. LAC Cooper died that same day in Conishead Military Hospital, Ulverston. Sgt Pilot Elliott is buried in Barrow Cemetery.

August, 1942 began with the funeral of Sgt Elliott on a dull and dismal day and because of these combined factors flying had been cancelled. I am sure that his death and the frequent failing of the Defiants must have affected station morale and given many of the brave, young airmen pause for thought as they paraded at the graveside.

On the 14th of August, around noon, a Junkers 88 was spotted above the airfield and all ground gunners stood to. The Junkers continued across the Duddon estuary and carried out a swift hit and run attack on RAF Millom. Using cannon and machine gun fire, but with no bombs dropped they escaped in a south-easterly direction before the RAF Millom gun crews could fire a shot. No casualties and no significant damage were caused in the attack, though it was a reminder that the enemy were never far away.

The 15th and 16th of the month saw No.27 F/E/AG Course pass out, 29 successfully, though 6 failed the course and were transferred to other duties (unspecified). 40 pupils were also posted in to begin training as No.30 F/E/AG Course.

We have seen beyond doubt that the undercarriage of the Defiant was responsible for many of the accidents involving the type to date, but now engine failures began to come to the fore. At 15.45hrs on the 20th of August, 1942 P/O J.F. Mackie with pupil LAC G.A. Bradshaw took off from No.10 AGS in Defiant N3449 to carry out a gunnery exercise. Shortly after take-off, 1½ miles north-east of the airfield and over the Duddon Estuary, the aircraft suffered a complete engine failure resulting in a crash into the sea which drowned both men. The body of P/O Mackie was recovered from the sea at 19.30hrs that same day, though it would be 48 hours or more before the body of LAC Bradshaw was located. We can be sure that P/O Mackie did not even have time to raise the undercarriage of N3449 before men and machine struck the sea. One of the plane's undercarriage legs, wheel axle and tyre has become visible, standing erect above the sand from time to time. The wreck is well known by local fishermen, in an area of the sands they know as the 'hard acre'.

The 3rd of September was designated 'National Day of Prayer' and a service for all personnel was held in the station's No.2 Hanger. In the evening 50 personnel joined members of all other services and marched through Barrow to an enthusiastic reception by townsfolk.

The next day, however, it was back to business and the first of the month's Defiant crashes occurred. At 18.20hrs a Defiant (no number recorded) flown by Sgt Pilot Short and with pupil LAC Wright on board crashed upon landing, due once again to an undercarriage failure.

Yet again the Medical Officer was summoned to the station's kitchen on the 7th of September. He had no hesitation in condemning 70lbs of cabbage as "unfit for human consumption" – who on earth were their suppliers!?

The 9th of September saw yet another Defiant crash (no number recorded) when the aircraft of Sgt Pilot Molesworth suffered an undercarriage collapse upon landing. The pilot escaped without injury. This was followed on the 17th by yet another crash involving a Defiant undercarriage. The aircraft of Sgt Pilot Gray, with pupil LAC Lecky, had also crashed upon landing, due to a collapse of the landing gear.

The only other minor incident to mar the month occurred when one of the unit's Defiants came to grief after swinging off the runway and on to boggy ground. The two man crew escaped without injury. The month closed with the successful passing out of 59 pupils of F/E/AG Course No.31 and the posting in of 60 pupils to begin training as Course No.34.

The 3rd of October is significant in terms of training at RAF Walney as it was on that date that an intake of 60 pupils arrived to make up Course No.36. They were to be trained not as Flight Engineers/Air Gunners but as Wireless operator/Air Gunners instead, in line with RAF requirements.

Defiant crashes continued to be a prominent feature of October, 1942 with the first occurring on the 6th. T3943, piloted by Sgt Pilot Molesworth, overshot on landing and ran off the runway end causing considerable damage

Photo Andy Thomas

N3328 whilst in frontline service with 151 Squadron.
The only Defiant ever with shark's teeth decoration.

to the airframe but leaving him uninjured. This was to be followed on the 9th when at 16.45hrs a Defiant suffered an undercarriage collapse on landing (number not recorded). There were no injuries to pilot W/O Hatchard and the machine was deemed repairable at the unit.

Given the constant rate of Defiant accidents it was inevitable that replacement aircraft would need to be ferried in to meet flying training requirements. One such replacement was to be Defiant N3328. Based at No.1 Air Armament School and it was being ferried to No.10 AGS RAF Walney, on the 24th of October, by F/Sgt Goulter RAAF.

During the delivery flight and just before noon the aircraft entered a severe hail storm, stalled and spun into the ground near Lower Clough Farm, Barnoldswick, Yorkshire, killing F/Sgt Goulter instantly. With the aircraft overdue it was assumed that an accident had occurred, but it was not until 18.00hrs that day that the crash was reported. Owing to very bad weather conditions, it was not until later the next day that the wreck was located and the pilot's remains brought back to RAF Walney. F/Sgt Goulter is buried in Barrow Cemetery.

F/Sgt Goulter RAAF

The situation was to be compounded yet further when, on the 27th October, the station suffered two more Defiant crashes, both the result of undercarriage problems. The first of these was to V1114 when the machine's starboard wheel flew off as P/O Pietrowski came in to land; he was uninjured. The second involved N4060 flown by Sgt Pilot Hughes. Having just touched down upon the runway, the aircraft's starboard undercarriage leg broke away from the Defiant completely causing the aircraft to spin down the landing strip and badly damage the airframe. Incredibly, Sgt Pilot Hughes escaped relatively unscathed from his machine.

November, 1942 brought very poor weather and problems with the unit's Boulton Paul Defiants continued unabated. The month's first crash being on the 9th when N3335 crashed following an undercarriage failure. Sgt Pilot

Ground crew service Defiant N1621 location unknown (not Walney). Photo Graham Pitchfork

Slade was uninjured. Three days later N1741 made a forced landing at RAF Squires Gate where the problem was deemed sufficiently serious as to warrant a complete engine change.

The very next day an undercarriage failure led to the crash of N3428. Sgt Pilot Hynes was uninjured. A day later, Sgt Pilot Ridgers escaped injury when he was forced to make a one wheel landing due to the fact that only one undercarriage leg would fully deploy on Defiant N1578.

The month closed with the passing out of 51 successful pupils of WOP/AG Course No.40 (flight engineers). Additionally, there was the induction of 45 cadets who would form Course No.43.

December proved to be a bitterly cold month with stiff winds and frequent sleet showers making flying unpleasant at times. The month, however, began without serious incident until a Defiant crash on the 12th. This was again due to undercarriage problems but with no injuries to crew recorded.

Due to the coastal location of RAF Walney, consideration had to be given to formulating some kind of strategy for Air-Sea rescue procedures. To this end, the unit was visited on the 16th of the month, by Squadron Leader Nicoll (Flying training Command), F/Offr Kerrison (Air Ministry) and S/ Ldr Kennedy (HQ 15 Group) who also inspected the unit and left the same day.

On the 27th of December, 1942 just after 13.00hrs, a report was received at RAF Millom that a Fairey Swordfish torpedo bomber had been seen flying very low over the Duddon Estuary and had been heard to crash into the sea. RAF Millom's ambulance was dispatched to the shoreline, but no sign of the wreck was to be seen. Conditions were very poor that day with a rapidly thickening fog and so help was requested from RAF Walney. In response to this F/Sgt Green with Cpl Vic Shirley took off from No.10 AGS in Lysander T1674 and began a search. In the ever increasing fog and flying at very low level, F/Sgt Green must have become disorientated resulting in them crashing into the woods above the Knott, just outside Millom.

I knew Mr Shirley personally and he told me that he remembered nothing of the actual crash, but the aircraft had caught fire when they hit the wood and he and his pilot were rendered unconscious. When he regained his senses the fire had luckily all but extinguished itself and he recalls seeing Mr Tyson, the local farmer, approaching the wreck to help them both out. The two airmen were taken to RAF Millom's Sick Quarters where they both made a speedy recovery.

Cpl Vic Shirley

The missing Swordfish was being flown from 772 Squadron Machirihanish to Sealand by Royal Naval pilot Sub/Lt Hewitt. Over the next few days, parts of the Swordfish began to wash up on the shoreline at Haverigg, but no trace of the pilot could be found. It would be several weeks before the sea gave up his body.

In the early 1990's Millom's coastguard were alerted to the fact that a bomb had been washed ashore between Haverigg and Silecroft. When they arrived at the scene they found that it was actually a torpedo. The outer casing had decayed away exposing the explosive charge, which having begun to dry out was fizzing and sputtering in a very alarming way! The Army Bomb Disposal Team were called and the device blown up in situ as a matter of urgency. I have wondered over the years if the Swordfish was the source of this device as I can find no record of torpedo usage on Millom's Duddon or Silecroft bombing ranges - we shall never know.

As the year drew to a close it is as though the Defiant had to have one final prang with which to close proceedings! On the 30th of December, the last Defiant crash of the year occurred, caused not surprisingly by an undercarriage failure. No serial number for this aircraft or crew names are recorded. It is as though the officer recording had just given up. Who can blame him!

Cpl Saunders, drogue operator
Photo Peter Yuile

Drogue operators LAC Flynn (left) with unknown pal and Martinet aircraft

No.10 Air Gunners School
RAF Walney Island, Barrow-in-Furness
Photo taken April 1942
Labelling by P.Yuile

CHAPTER FOUR

1943
The Unit Comes To Operational Strength

During the latter part of 1942, not only was the station fulfilling its training commitment, it was also steadily being brought up to its prescribed strength. At the outset of 1943 this stood at 67 Officers, 144 NCOs, 818 Corporals and Airmen plus a WAAF contingent of 5 Officers, 10 NCOs and 371 Airwomen. Training courses had now become larger with a course of some 60 pupils not uncommon.

Command of No.10 AGS changed on the 1st of January, when W/Cdr Giles handed over to Group Captain M.L. Heath. It also saw the unit brace itself for another cold and blustery winter with nothing between them and the westerly gales whipping in from the Irish Sea.

January is significant for two other reasons. Firstly, that we only see one Defiant crash recorded on the 15th with the usual undercarriage failure (V1139; crew uninjured). The second reason is that it is at this point we begin to see the arrival of Miles Martinets as replacement target towing aircraft and Avro Ansons as gun platforms for gunnery pupils. The Defiant's days at last were numbered and as one veteran Anson pilot told me, "At least when you put an Anson's wheels down, they usually stayed down!"

Miles Martinet. Photo Ken Ellis

Avro Anson

A tragic start was made to February, on the 1st of the month, at 17.25hrs. Following a loss of control whilst carrying out a gunnery exercise, Defiant N3507 dived into the ground, bursting into flames and killing Sgt Pilot J. Blunden, and his pupil LAC D. Wilson. Tragedy was only narrowly avoided once again on the 8th when the station's ORB records that *"A Defiant aircraft taxied in front of another Defiant Aircraft which was in the act of taking off and the two collided. The pilot of the first aircraft, F/Sgt Short, and LAC Smith, received no injuries. The pilot of the second aircraft, Sgt O'Neill, also received no injuries, but LAC Hale, his gunner, received a small cut on the forehead requiring one suture."* As the photograph taken in the aftermath of the incident clearly shows, both crews were fortunate in the extreme to escape their respective wrecks without very serious injury.

The next day the station was the scene of an emergency landing by Blackburn Botha W5122 of No.11 RS (Radio School). The aircraft had suffered a starboard engine failure out over the Irish Sea and was forced to carry out a 'belly landing' as the loss of the engine left insufficient hydraulic pressure with which to lower the undercarriage. The pilot and his three crewmen were uninjured.

The Botha had earned itself a fearsome reputation during its short career as an aircraft which was not to be trusted, with engine failures suffered by the type very common indeed. This resulted in many fatal and near fatal crashes with the Botha featuring very prominently across the country in airfield records as forced landings. Surprisingly then, the W5122 'belly landing' is the only one of two recorded instances of a Botha in trouble using RAF Walney's runways for the entire span of the station's life.

On the 11th of February, concerns began to be expressed when Lysander V9666 became long overdue on its expected return from an early morning flying detail. At 09.00hrs the station received a call to say that a Lysander aircraft had been seen to dive into the sea close to Fleetwood and just off the Whyre Point Lighthouse. With the station's fears confirmed, a search by sea and air was mounted for the missing crew, Sgt Pilot Szot, and his drogue operator, LAC Jolly. The search was to no avail and after several days it was scaled

Walney Defiant N1679 following collison (8/2/43)

down and subsequently abandoned; the bodies of Sgt Pilot Szot and LAC Jolly were never found.

At 17.22hrs on the very next day, the Defiant (no number recorded) of Sgt Pilot Norton and his pupil LAC Habbershow sustained a burst tyre on take-off forcing an immediate return and an emergency landing, fortunately executed perfectly and without incident.

Due to aircraft lost from strength the station must have been desperate for

10 AGS station Sick Quarters staff 1943

and eagerly awaiting the arrival of Defiant N1551 which was being ferried to them that day as Air Transport Auxiliary flight No.6 FPP. They were to be disappointed!

Following an engine failure, ATA Pilot Reisert (an American) had 'bailed out' of the machine which crashed near Lindal-in-Furness. The pilot landed safely at what was at the time High Carley Sanatorium on the outskirts of Ulverston. The station's Medical Officer attended the scene as a matter of routine, though can barely have done so before he was called to yet another crash in the locality.

The Dalton-in-Furness police rang the unit at 12.52hrs to say that an aircraft had crashed at Poaka Beck, just north of Marton village. The aircraft was a Beaufighter, and upon attending the scene it was obvious that nothing could be done for the crew. S/Ldr Alexandrowicz and P/Offr Domanski had both died instantly as a result of the impact.

It was on the 21st of February that the first recorded accident involving one of the unit's newly acquired Martinets occurred. It was to be the first of two that month. A Martinet (no number recorded) ran off the runway and became bogged down on the grass, causing the machine to 'nose over', wrecking propeller and engine but leaving its pilot (Sgt J.Evans) unharmed. The second accident occurred to a Martinet flown by Sgt Pilot Sawoszczyk who was forced to crash land his aircraft following an engine failure. The landing was executed successfully into an open field close to Hawcoat Golf Course and once again the pilot was able to escape with little injury.

Far more spectacular was the crash which occurred on the airfield at 14.30hrs the next day. Upon returning from a gunnery exercise in Defiant AA299, its pilot, Sgt Pilot Hughes, discovered that he was unable to lower his undercarriage. After carrying our several circuits whilst trying to free the landing gear, he finally gave up and carried out a 'belly landing' on the airfield. As the aircraft slid down the runway trailing sparks and debris in its wake, it burst into flames before it had come to rest. Fortunately, Sgt Pilot Hughes

A foam covered AA299 following its successful belly-landing and subsequent fire which has clearly caused the starboard wing tank to explode. Photo courtesy of Mike Gill

LACW Marion Jackson

LACW Ethel Cunningham

These four WAAFs had been re-mustered from other duties to be re-trained as Flight mechanics/Airframe fitters. Joan, Ethel and Elsie had been barrage balloon operators. During this period a minister at the local Presbyterian church had set up a canteen in the church basement for all female forces. These WAAFs often enjoyed socialising there and it's where, in 1943, they first met Peter Yuile (who kindly provided much of the source material for this book) whose stepmother helped out in the canteen. After closing time he would often walk them back to the airfield through the blackout and they formed a friendship which has lasted down the years. All four WAAFs feature in pictures throughout this book.

LACW Joan Metcalfe

LACW Elsie Rhodes

and his pupil AC Johnson were able to leap to safety leaving the fire crews to tackle the, by now, flaming machine.

By the beginning of March, 1943 the WAAF contingent of No.10 AGS was almost up to strength and occupying their two sites down on North Scale. Most of these women would have been employed as Flight Mechanic/Airframes, or Flight Mechanic/Engines and a fair number of them would have been posted in on transfer from barrage balloon operation sites.

Second in charge of their training was Flt/Lt Jim Reason who went on to serve out in the Far East. At the close of hostilities Jim was responsible for the sending back of four Japanese aircraft to Britain for evaluation from Panang. They were delivered to the RAF's experimental and development unit at RAF Bascombe Down and are now held in preservation in the UK.

(L to R) ex Sqdn Ldr Jim Reason, LACW Elsie Rhodes, Mrs Reason & LACW Joan Gledhill (1980's reunion). Photo P.Yuile

On the east side of the WAAF sites was established a station piggery. It seems a unique initiative as neither RAF Millom, nor RAF Cark had such a thing. I'm sure that the bacon was welcome, but I'm also sure that the ladies must have prayed for the wind to stay from the west!

On the 11th of March, 1943 the station's Medical Officer was called to the beach at North Scale to investigate reports that human remains had been washed ashore there. A very badly decomposed body was recovered and conveyed to the station's mortuary where identification was established using a badly damaged, but legible pay book and identity discs. The sea had finally, after almost ten weeks, given up the body of Sub/Lt E. Hewitt who had perished in his swordfish aircraft on the 27th of December, the previous year.

The month was to cost the unit three more Defiants, two from undercarriage failures and one due to engine malfunction. The first accident occurred on the 15th and involved N1582 (no crew names recorded), due to an undercarriage collapse upon landing. The second, involving N3428 on the 19th (no crew names recorded) was again due to the failure of the machine's undercarriage on landing. It is amazing to think that, once again, both crews escaped with

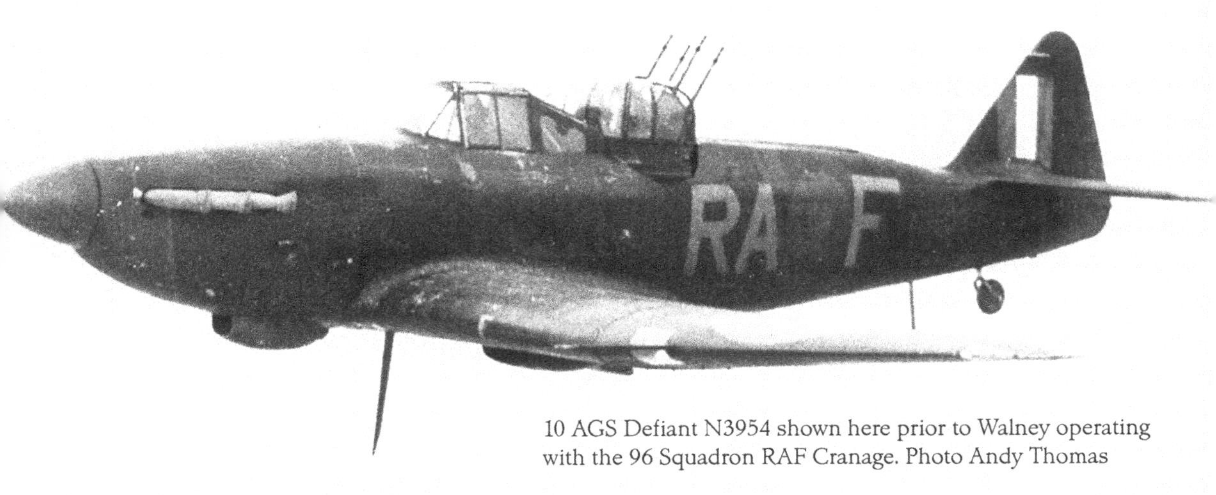

10 AGS Defiant N3954 shown here prior to Walney operating with the 96 Squadron RAF Cranage. Photo Andy Thomas

little injury. Defiant number three was lost to operational strength on the 27th when N3459 developed engine problems. P/Offr Woods (RCAF), along with his gunnery pupil LAC Meredith, made a forced landing on Biggar Bank, Walney Island, walking away from the incident with only bruises and minor abrasions.

On the 3rd of April, Barrow-in-Furness celebrated the start of 'Wings for Victory' week. No.10 AGS mustered WAAF and RAF personnel for a march through the town, accompanied by a pipe band that had flown in from RAF Jurby on the Isle of Man to mark the occasion. The salute was taken by the Marshall of the Royal Air Force, Sir Edward Ellington.

Along with the obvious training duties and commitments demanded of the unit, airfield security and defence was no less of a priority. In order to test the efficacy of the latter, various agencies would be engaged to mount a mock attack on the airfield. Often, this would be members of the Home Guard, but also might involve the Territorial Army or any units who might be in the locality and available at the time. On the 11th of April, a ferocious attack was launched upon the unit by the 11th Argyll and Sutherland Highlanders. Not ferocious enough though, as it recorded that they were repelled, leaving the RAF as clear victors!

The weather for April was poor to say the very least with flying taking place as and when conditions allowed. Also of note, is the fact that around this time the troublesome Defiants are being steadily flown out to other units (including maintenance units) and more reliable Avro Ansons flown in as their replacements. Along with this, the Lysander was also being superseded by the Miles Martinet as the station's main target towing aircraft, a role for which it was specifically designed.

Sadly April, like the month before it, was to see three more Defiants lost from station strength due to crashes. The first of these involved N1630 (no crew names recorded) which overshot in very poor visibility resulting in extensive damage to the airframe, but leaving both crewmen uninjured.

The second incident began as a coolant leak on the engine of N1735 whilst it was engaged on a gunnery exercise out on the target ranges. This forced a swift return and an emergency landing which should have been a safe and straightforward solution to a minor problem. However, upon landing, the Defiant's undercarriage suffered a total collapse, causing sufficient damage to the machine as to render it beyond the capacity of the unit to repair. Once again, the two men on board (no crew names recorded) escaped with nothing more than minor cuts and bruises from a serious incident which was, by this time, becoming a regular occurrence.

The month was crowned by the loss of the station's third Defiant on the 28th of April. Defiant T4074 suffered a total engine failure at sea over the south Lancashire coast. Fortunately, the tide was out and the pilot was able to glide in for a forced landing on the sands near Fleetwood. Upon touching down, however, the aircraft burst into flames. Necessitating a swift exit by pilot and pupil (no crew names recorded), it was carried out safely and once again, incredibly, resulted in little or no injury to either man. This was yet another fortunate escape from an accident involving an aircraft that was earning itself a reputation as a machine which was not to be trusted.

60 pupils of No.57 Air Gunnery Course passed out successfully on the 8th of May. Four days later all flying in the airfield ceased for a day as various exercises involving the station's defence against a gas attack were carried out. These involved the decontamination of an area where a poison gas shell had been detonated in a controlled explosion. Time was also spent in the Army mobile gas training vehicle which had been brought to the unit for the

10 AGS Defiant N1744 seen here on operational duties prior to Walney with 256 squadron RAF Woodvale. Photo Andy Thomas

Wellington crash Rampside. Photo NW Evening Mail

occasion. This involved spending two minutes in a gas filled chamber with a gas mask on, then two minutes exposed to the gas without a mask. I am told that the Army instructors enjoyed this training immensely. The recipients of the training, conversely, did not!

The 16th of May brought yet another Defiant crash (no aircraft number recorded) and no clear reasons given for what the unit's log records as a "crash landing". It is probably fair to assume that an undercarriage failure was the culprit once again. However, the two man crew, Sgt Scorgie, and his pupil LAC Phipps, were able to leave the crash with no injuries sustained. Once again, this was a fortunate outcome to a potentially dangerous incident.

On the 20th of the month, a distress call was received from the pilot of a Miles Magister, outbound from RAF Thame (pilot's name and destination not recorded). The aircraft was suffering engine problems which became so severe that the pilot was forced to land his aircraft in the sea some distance off the Furness coast. A successful rescue was carried out by Barrow's lifeboat and the pilot was treated in RAF Walney's Sick Quarters for minor injuries, before being flown back to his parent unit.

Four days later on the 24th of May, RAF Walney was the scene of a dramatic crash involving one of the unit's target towing Martinets. After lifting off from the station's east/west runway the aircraft, HP135, inexplicably swung violently to starboard and crashed, shearing off the undercarriage and overturning. Fortunately, no fire was ignited in the crash and given the circumstances the crew escaped with quite minor, if painful, injuries. Sgt Pilot Fenner suffered displaced cartilage in his right knee and his winch man, AC/I King, was treated for a gash on his left knee - it was their lucky day!

Two further crashes occurred on the 27th of May and they are significant in that they are the last accidents involving Boulton Paul Defiant aircraft that the station would record. The Defiant had been all but banished from RAF Walney's runways by now and it is difficult to imagine any aircrew mourning its passing.

The first crash took place at 08.37hrs and can be attributed to the usual undercarriage failure (no aircraft number or crew names recorded), and once again, the occupants escaped with cuts and bruises. The second crash of the day, however, took the lives of Sgt Pilot J.B.J. Methven, and his pupil gunner, LAC Hosh. The cause of the crash was never established but was presumed to be the result of a spin following a steep turn. Whatever the cause, Defiant V1173 - the last of its type to be lost to the unit - tore into the ground near Yarlside Mines, Roose, killing both young crewmen and spreading wreckage over a large area.

To further cast a shadow over a unit still keenly feeling the loss of these men, two more crashes occurred on the 31st of May. This time it was as the result of a mid-air collision and once again resulted in fatalities. Whilst engaged in a gunnery exercise, Avro Anson LT778 collided with Martinet HP303 out at sea over the station's target range. This resulted in a total loss of control for the pilot of the Anson and the aircraft plunged into the beach half a mile west of the airfield killing all on board. They were Sgt Pilot Anderton, F/O Creed (inst), LAC Wilson, LAC Hudson and LAC Lanaghan. The pilot of the Martinet was more fortunate, however, though his aircraft was significantly damaged, he was uninjured and was able to make an emergency landing at the airfield. It had been a sobering month for the unit and one I am sure that everyone would have been glad to put behind them.

June brought three further crashes, although one of them did not involve a Walney aircraft. On the 20th the station's Medical Officer was called to attend a crashed Wellington aircraft at Rampside. The aircraft's flaps had become locked whilst it was undergoing an air test and a crash landing was made between the Clarkes Arms Public House and Foulney Island. I have been unable to discover where the Wellington was flying from and no number is visible on the rear fuselage. The aircraft does, however, appear to be painted in coastal command colours. Additionally, the fact that those posing with the airframe during recovery are Vickers Aero Works staff, it is possible that the aircraft had yet to be allocated to a unit. The only injuries recorded were suffered by the pilot who sustained sprained wrists.

The month was marked by very variable weather from the outset, with windy and wet conditions predominating – a far cry from the melting runways of June, 1942! It is interesting that the two other crashes of the station's aircraft this month both involve undercarriage failures. Although, on these occasions they occurred to Martinet HP271 on the 11th of June and Miles Master (no aircraft number recorded) on the 22nd. No crew names or injuries are recorded for either incident.

One wonders if the winds to which the airfield is exposed were a contributory factor given the inordinate number of undercarriage problems experienced by RAF Walney. I think that it is entirely possible that those strong winds and gusty, blustery conditions may have given rise to many 'heavier than normal' arrivals. Whatever the reasons for such troubles, the Operational Record Books for RAF Millom and RAF Cark do not speak of undercarriage problems to the same extent. This is telling, as these units were flying the same types of aircraft as RAF Walney, in what were broadly speaking, the same roles.

Merciful respite from the trials and tragedies of previous months came with July. With the exception of a minor taxying accident involving Anson LT788 – which resulted in only superficial damage to the aircraft following a collision with a refuelling unit – the month was to pass without serious incident.

With the coming of August, the weather on the Lancashire and Cumberland coast became very changeable and on the night of the 8th it became dangerous in the extreme. Due to RAF Walney's specific training role, little or no night flying details were carried out. This was not the case, however, for units where Air Observers or Navigators were under training.

On any given night large numbers of aircraft from various stations would be flying over the Lake District, the Welsh Mountains and the Irish Sea. At dusk on the 8th of August, the crews of various units boarded their aircraft for what should have been quite routine training flights, having been given a reasonably good meteorological forecast at their pre-flight briefings. It was subsequently officially recorded that this forecast was grossly inaccurate, though the ferocity of the weather system which struck in the early hours of the 9th could surely not have been fully anticipated. Those who remember the night in question have spoken to me of tremendously strong winds, hail storms, lightning strikes on aircraft and the rapid and violent onset of this freak weather event.

At around 01.15hrs on the 9th, RAF Walney intercepted a very broken distress call from an unidentified aircraft somewhere close by and the station readied its runways for the arrival of emergency landings - none were received. As dawn broke searches were mounted for aircraft reported missing from their units. It was discovered that no less than four aircraft had crashed upon the Lake District fells. RAF Millom's Mountain Rescue unit located the wreck of Anson DJ275 high up on the rocks of Cam Spout, below the summit of Scafell. The aircraft was flying a night navigational exercise from 10 OAFU, RAF Dumfries, and the five men on board all perished in the crash. In addition to this, Dumfries lost a further two Ansons to the fells that night; DJ229 was found on Green Gable and N5053 on Great Dodd. The fourth Anson was L5986 of 3 OAFU, RAF Babbington, which was found to have crashed at Carrock Beck, Heskit, with its crew having survived the accident. One member of aircrew lost his life in the Great Dodd crash and a further two on Green Gable. It had been a disastrous night and one which stretched rescue teams to their limits.

RAF Walney was to lose a second of its newly acquired Avro Ansons, on the 18th of August, when LT767 suffered a complete failure of its port engine at low altitude, five miles offshore from Blackpool. The crew (no names are recorded) were able to abandon their aircraft safely following a successful 'ditching'. They were rescued in their dinghy by Fleetwood Lifeboat some time later and then returned to RAF Walney uninjured.

Blackpool was the scene of further drama on the 23rd of the month, when the engine of Martinet HP271 suddenly failed and the pilot was forced to carry out an emergency landing (no crew names recorded). The aircraft came to rest safely in a field three miles north-west of Blackpool, on the outskirts of Hadthorne village, where the pilot and his crewman were picked up by personnel from nearby RAF Squires Gate and flown back to their unit at RAF Walney.

By the 29th of August, the station was recording appalling weather conditions with visibility reduced to less than 1,000 yards at times and flying frequently cancelled. This poor weather persisted throughout September, 1943. It must have adversely affected flying commitments as the unit's ORB contains little in the way of entries for the whole of that month. The exceptions to this being the entries for the passing out of No.69, No.70 and No.71 Courses of WOP/AG's, and the induction of No.74 Course to begin training.

Only two noteworthy incidents are recorded for October, 1943, both of which occurred on the 22nd of the month. At approximately 10.10hrs a

Unamed group posed on Walney sand dunes

No.1 Hangar, Ground Crew squad 'NAAFI up!' (front row left Ethel Cunningham)

collision occurred between Martinets HP273 and HP307 causing extensive damage to both machines though with both crews escaping serious injury (no crew names recorded). Just after lunch the same day, the station's log records that an Avro Tutor biplane (K4837), which had been performing aerobatics over the airfield, made a swift and safe landing. This followed the fracture of its rudder main spar which occurred whilst the pilot was executing a tight loop. It is not recorded whether the Tutor was a visiting aircraft, or perhaps a requisitioned one for use as a station transport, but it is never mentioned in the unit's records before this event or indeed afterwards.

It is indicative of how poor the autumn weather had been that comment is made, at the beginning of November, about a vast improvement. The unit's safety record was undeniably improved also with only two forced landings throughout the whole month. One of these was Martinet HP274 on the 13th, following an engine failure. The other, Anson LT765, on the 22nd, was due to the pilot finding that he was unable to deploy the aircraft's undercarriage (no crew names recorded).

The 22nd of November also saw a great deal of activity on the station. A welcoming parade was mustered for the arrival of Prince Bernhard of the Netherlands who flew in with his escort from RAF Hendon to visit Messrs Vickers-Armstrongs Ltd. The Prince remained in the town overnight and was flown back to Hendon the next day.

The year was drawing to a close and on the 5th of December, Course No.80 arrived to begin their training. At this point in its service life the unit had trained somewhere in the region of 5,028 Air Gunners and Engineers, a record of which the unit could be justifiably proud. The station's ORB does not record what festivities took place for station personnel over the Christmas period, but does state that on the 22nd of December, L/Ldr D.F.C. Mills played the role of Santa for the unit staff children.

The year, however, was to end on a tragic note. At 13.00hrs following a suspected engine failure, F/Sgt Pilot E.H. Ciurkot (Polish Forces). and LAC Collins, his target towing operator, attempted to make an emergency landing on Biggar Bank near Biggar village. This resulted in a crash in which LAC Collins died instantly. F/Sgt Ciurkot was recovered alive from the wreckage of Martinet JN493, but succumbed to his injuries a short time later. F/Sgt Ciurkot is buried in Barrow-in-Furness Cemetery.

F/Sgt Pilot E.H. Ciurkot

CHAPTER FIVE

1944
The Arrival of Wellingtons at 10AGS

On the 1st of January 1944, Martinet HP303, flown by W/O Pyka, crashed upon landing due to an undercarriage failure. As a consequence of this, all Martinet aircraft were grounded by the unit's Chief Technical Officer in order to investigate the repeated hydraulic failures.

RAF Walney now had a newly completed station theatre. And, on the 5th of January, RAF Cark's concert party performed a show called 'Happy Landings' to much applause. The notion of happy landings must have been close to the hearts of those flying the ailing Martinets.

The problems associated with these grounded aircraft appear to have been resolved, as they were back in the skies within a couple of days. However, the next incident involving this type was on the 14th of the month, this time in the form of a collision between PH285 and HP287 (no crew manes or injuries recorded).

The station's theatre was packed once again on the 14th when RAF Walney's very own and newly formed concert party performed their very own show, appropriately entitled 'Wind and Rain'.

Both photos - LACWs Elsie Hogg & Ethel Cunningham
10 AGS No.1 Hangar with C.O's hack Miles Magister T9768
Photo: P.Yuile

By the 18th of January, the weather was once again very poor. Visibility was reduced to such a degree that Martinet HP314 (no crew names recorded), was forced to make an emergency landing on Cockerham Sands on the South Lancashire coast. Fortunately, this was completed successfully, resulting in little damage to the aircraft and no injuries to her crew.

At 30 minutes past noon, on the 23rd of January, an airman was found in a hypothermic state, in the road, at Biggar Bank and was taken to a house close by. He was in fact the pilot of Anson F4 of RAF Cranage, which had been lost at sea two days previously due to engine failure. P/O Whittaker had ditched off Anglesey and managed to board the aircraft emergency dinghy along with his three man crew. After two days at sea he was the only survivor. When their dinghy was located where they had washed ashore near Biggar village, F/Sgt Wright, Sgt Wise and Sgt Davey, were all found to have perished from exposure. It remains a miracle that P/O Whittaker managed to survive two days at sea, in the cruel January conditions, in an open craft. At Biggar Village Whittaker met the Swarbrick sisters (who raised the alarm) whose father was the lighthouse keeper on Walney. Peggy Swarbrick would go on to be the only woman principal lighthouse-keeper in Britain for which she earned an MBE.

By the 25th of the month, heavy rain and gales had set in, and flying was suspended until the 27th. At 11.10hrs that day, Martinet HP309 and HP310 were in collision with each other whilst taxying. The crash was a spectacular one! It is recorded that the fuselage of HP309 was cut completely in two! Incredibly, no injuries are recorded as a result of this mishap, which

'A' Flight ground crew pose (above) on battle command HQ and (below) outside crew hut.

('A' Flight's dog was later unfortunately killed by jumping up at a revolving Anson propellor.)

can only be ascribed to very good fortune! On board HP310, were Sgt Pilot Collins and LAC Booth, whilst on board HP309, were F/Sgt McEwen and Sgt Johnson.

By this stage of the war, many captured Italian prisoners were being held in camps in the United Kingdom. One such camp was sited in Milnthorpe. On the 1st of February, RAF Walney's Station Commander, Group Captain Heath, accompanied by Squadron Leader Evans, travelled to Milnthorpe to discuss the possibility of employing Italian prisoners of war to help cultivate crops with which to provision the station. An agreement was reached with the Commandant of the camp and accommodation was made available, adjacent to the airfield, pending the arrival of the first Italian 'co-operators'. This arrangement was by no means unusual, a smaller prisoner of war camp was in existence at Silecroft and a number of Italian workers were at that time employed at RAF Millom.

'C' Flight 10 AGS Miles Martinet TT1 (north end of airfield)

Only one incident was to mar the month when one of the unit's Ansons suffered an undercarriage collapse upon landing (no aircraft number or crew names are recorded). A frequent cause of high ground crashes was a situation where a pilot was lost in bad visibility and attempted to descend below cloud to establish his position. This appears to have been the cause of the crash of Martinet HP311, flown by Sgt Pilot TH Allen, who was killed instantly when his aircraft struck a hill above Fairbank, Kendal, in cloudy conditions on the morning of the 18th of March. This was to be the last accident or incident for some ten weeks, with April and May seeing the station enjoying a period of routine trouble-free operation. The first such respite since the unit's formation.

On the 2nd of June, 317 Squadron ATC (Newton Heath) arrived at the station to begin a week's camp. This activity was eagerly anticipated by all young cadets as it presented the opportunity to take to the air, usually in one of the unit's Avro Ansons. 317 Squadron were the first of several Lancashire ATC groups to visit throughout the summer.

For many months the Furness skies had been clear of enemy aircraft. On the 27th of June, however, the anti-aircraft gun crews of No.10 AGS were called to their stations at 12.15hrs, following reports of German aircraft having been spotted out at sea. The air raid warning proved a false alarm and the gun crews were stood down at 12.42hrs. A further air raid warning was sounded at 13.05hrs and once again the unit's gunners took to their posts, only to be stood down once more at 13.42hrs. Wherever the reported aircraft were headed, Barrow at least had been spared their attentions.

The next day, all sections took part in the station's sports day. After fierce competition, RAF Walney's servicing wing was the outright winner of the sports cup!

Flying throughout July was repeatedly hampered by bad weather, though no accidents or incidents occurred as a result, until the 28th of the month. At 13.00hrs that day, P/O Dumbleton, in Martinet HP311, failed to return from a flying detail and was posted as missing. Following a search by aircraft from the unit, the wreck of HP311 was found high up on Corney Fell, near Stoneside Hill. The P/O had perished in the crash and his body was recovered by RAF Millom's Mountain Rescue team later that same day.

Visibility was poor at the time of the accident and it is possible that the aircraft struck the high ground as a result of this. Even so, the station's ORB records no official opinions as to the cause of the crash. An eyewitness who saw the wreck of the aircraft at the time described to me a steep angle entry into relatively level, soft ground which makes one wonder if engine failure of some description, was once again the culprit. The location

Drogue operators & packers 10 AGS

Summer at 10 AGS! front row middle Wally Smith, pre-war manager of the Co-op Powerful St, Barrow.

of the crash site, however, does seem to suggest that the pilot was lost.

On the 31st of July, the unit's Medical Officer met with Barrow-in-Furness water supply overseers and the station's Chief Engineer, when it was discovered that the airfield's drinking water supply was seriously contaminated. No illness had been reported as result of this, though the level of contamination was unacceptable. The cause was found to be foul water run-off from the piggeries. Subsequently, steps were taken to prevent this. In addition, the unit's water, from that point on, was to be chlorinated at source.

Command of No.10 AGS was about to change and the 9th of August, 1944 saw Grp/Cpt L.R.S. Freestone, OBE, arrive on station in a supernumerary capacity pending his taking overall command of the unit. The only other noteworthy item recorded for the month is logged on the 25th. We are told that Anson LT644 (no crew names recorded), was in collision with trees on the outskirts of Barrow whilst low flying. It is very unlikely that this 'low flying' was officially sanctioned, though no follow up disciplinary action is mentioned in subsequent entries.

On the 9th of September, RAF Walney's Senior Medical Officer made the following entry, "A case of Misnetic Pseudo-Cyesis has been admitted to our Sick Quarters, the airman is on leave from RAF Henlow. There are no abdominal signs whatever, but he complains of acute abdominal pain. He has apparently miscalculated since his wife is not due for another month yet!"

A phantom pregnancy! A most novel way to avoid returning from your leave! Clearly, the SM/O was having none of it. However, it appears that the Henlow airman had no intentions of returning to his unit either, for on the 29th of September the SM/O made the following wry entry, "The case of the 9/9/44 has been re-admitted from Barrow Police Station. His pregnancy is now further complicated by the early expectation of an RAF escort!"

Following this levity, however, the month was to end in tragedy. On the 30th of September whilst returning to the airfield from a gunnery exercise, Anson LT532 struck the steel drogue cable of a Miles Master as it was also making its return to base. As a result of this the Anson's starboard wing was sheared off and the aircraft plunged into allotments close to Avon Strait, Walney Island, killing all on board. They were F/Sgt Jordan, Sgt Cooke and Sgt Conisbee. The Miles Master and its pilot made a safe landing back at the unit.

By this time in the airfield's history the troublesome Boulton Paul Defiant aircraft had been totally replaced by the more reliable Avro Ansons as gunships. As a result the unit's accident rate had dropped in a dramatic and sustained way, though as the crash of the 30th clearly demonstrated, human error would always be a factor. It must be remembered also, that the machines being flown were worked very hard indeed, which coupled with the exposed conditions on Walney, rendered the aircraft vulnerable to structural and engine failures. A prime example of this was an accident on the 2nd of October when the port engine of Anson LT777 failed on take-off causing the aircraft to swing and the undercarriage to fail (no crew names or injuries recorded).

No.10 AGS 1944.
(Top row 2nd left Bob Drummond, Second row, 1st left Stan Groves, Second row 2nd left Taff Evans. All three men were posted to Lancaster Squadrons and survived the war)

By 1944, all military aircraft carried on board a transmitter system for use when the aircraft and crew were in difficulty, or distress. This system would transmit the code word "DARKY". The device had a range of around ten miles and all airfields operated a receiver. Should an aircraft transmit on the darky frequency then the receiving station would know the approximate location of the aircraft within a ten mile radius. It was a valuable life saver for many crews, though sadly not in the following instance.

At 19.50hrs on the 22nd of October, 1944 RAF Millom intercepted a darky transmission from an aircraft in distress. That aircraft was Halifax LL505, S-Sugar which was out from RAF Topcliffe in Yorkshire on a night navigational exercise. RAF Millom's response was immediate. In view of the Lake District Mountains close by, the pilot of S-Sugar was instructed to circle at his present position and to maintain an altitude of no less than 4,000 feet. This message was not acknowledged by the crew of LL505 and it is obvious that they did not receive it. At 20.00hrs RAF Walney was alerted to the emergency and they dispatched an aircraft to attempt close enough proximity to the Halifax to enable radio contact to be made. Also seeking LL505 was a Mosquito aircraft from RAF Church Fenton in Yorkshire, who had also received the bombers distress transmission as the aircraft passed within their range. It was all to no avail. At around 20.20hrs, in bad visibility and flying on a north-west to south-easterly heading, the Halifax tore into the upper flank of Great Carrs, Coniston, at an impact altitude of 2,250 feet. The aircraft first struck some 50 feet below the summit of the fell, sliding uphill, coming to rest and burning out on the crest of the ridge killing all eight crewmen on board. The Halifax crew were, F/O J.Armstrong Johnston, F/O F.Aubrey Bell, F/O R.Newton Whitley, Sgt C.G.Whitingstall, Sgt G.Riddock, Sgt D.F. Titt, Sgt W.B.Ferguson and Sgt H.Pyche. It was to take two days for RAF Millom's Mountain Rescue team to complete the awful task of recovering the bodies of these young men. The tragedy was a sobering reminder, if one were needed, of the dangerously high ground that lay just a few miles inland.

The weather, already bad at the time of the Halifax crash, became increasingly poor over the ensuing days, causing the cancellation of flying on a regular basis. Conditions had improved somewhat by the 28th of October, when the unit received its first Vickers Wellington aircraft, a MKIII serial X3414. This was to be the first of several such arrivals. This forerunner was to allow the WAAF and RAF airframe and engine fitters to familiarise themselves with the type, ahead of further Wellington's being ferried in.

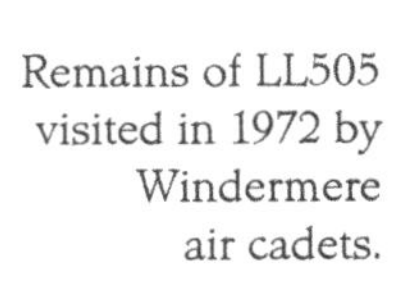

Remains of LL505 visited in 1972 by Windermere air cadets.

Photo: Martin Wyness (pictured in foreground)

A team of prison staff recover the undertail section of S for Sugar's fuselage on a foul day in 1997.

Photo: John Nixon

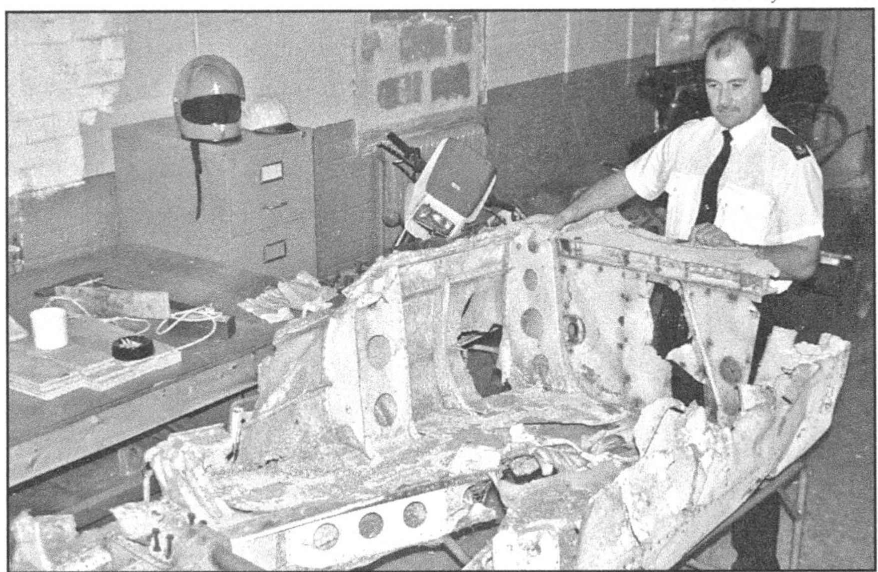

The author John Nixon with the undertail section of LL505 in HM Prison Haverigg's aircraft restoration workshop following its recovery.

Graeme Brass with fuselage portion of LL505.
Autumn 2007

John Nixon with control surface hinge of LL505.
Autumn 2007

'he view down Greenburn with portion of now widely dispersed wreckage in foreground

John Nixon at memorial to LL505,
summit of Great Carrs Winter 2008

A Rolls Royce Merlin engine from Halifax LL505
currently outside the Ruskin Museum in Coniston.

Pictured with the engine is Philippa Tuck (née Wrathall). Her father, Corporal D.E. Wrathall was part of the Millom team that attended the crash.

RAF Millom's mountain rescue team with Humber ambulance and Jeep 1944.

November 9th 1944
A Tragedy For 10AGS and a Mystery of the Sands.

What follows is a story which has haunted, frustrated and confounded me since I had it first told to me by my father as a young boy. It is the story of an airman and his aircraft lost in the sands of the Leven Estuary on the above date that remain where they crashed to the present day.

The aircraft was on a test flight from 10 AGS Walney and was a Miles Martinet flown by W/Off Pyka, a Polish pilot who had been posted to Walney from 10 OAFU Dumfries. I have in my records three accounts of the incident and how it was dealt with and because two of them contradict each other I decided to devote some deep research into the matter with a view to establishing hard facts.

We must begin by looking at the three versions of this event as given to me, and then evaluate them using Admiralty Tidal Records and the station logs of RAF Walney and RAF Cark, which do provide a valuable time frame for the incident and its aftermath.

Account No. 1

During the war years my father worked on the family farm at Greenhurst which is situated on the fellside above Cartmel. My grandparents Martha and Thomas Nixon also took in bed and breakfast guests to supplement their income. The farm proved a welcome retreat for many staff from RAF Cark and a very regular visitor who became a close family friend was W/Off Ralph Room. It was from Ralph that my father was told the story of the crash out on the sands and his version of events was as follows:

Word had been received late in the afternoon of the 9th of November that an aircraft had been seen to crash offshore near Ulverston Railway viaduct. RAF Walney had received a distress call from one of its aircraft and suspected that the plane was indeed theirs. My father recalled that a search had taken place, but it was the next day before the wreck could be located. However, he could not remember on which side of the viaduct it was found.

W/Off Room told my father that the aircraft sank into the sand so fast, that divers were brought in to try and recover the pilot's body. But, it proved impossible and the aircraft became buried forcing all efforts to be abandoned after three days of continuous attempts to access the cockpit.

Account No. 2

This account of the incident was given to me first hand by Mr Vic Shirley who was a friend of W/Off Pyka and who was in post at Walney when the crash occurred. Vic told me:

"I was a serving Corporal (Aircrew) at 10 AGS Walney when Pyka crashed and I recall the version of events that we received very well. I was present the afternoon he took off and I remember that he was in civilian clothes, just about to go on leave when he was asked to perform an air test on a Martinet which had been in for a repair. He agreed to do this and we were told that shortly after take-off and a few miles from that airfield the aircraft shed its propeller, which forced him to crash land on the sands near Ulverston.

I recall that a search was mounted but it was next day that his plane was found partly buried in soft sand but with the cockpit empty. We all believed that he had survived the crash and tried to make for the shore, only to either be drowned by the tide or sucked under the quicksand. I do recall very clearly that his body was never found".

Account No. 3

The third and final version of the crash is concise and was given by W/Cdr Gibb to at least two sources who in turn have recounted it to me. There is no doubt that as Station Commander of RAF Cark, Jim Gibb was very "hands on" and would participate fully in all rescue operations both on site and when assistance was required further afield, so it is natural to assume that being the closest station to this crash he would automatically respond by attending with a rescue team. W/Cdr Gibbs version of the incident was as follows:

RAF Cark was notified of a crash out on the sands near the station and he took a team to search for the aircraft and pilot. Having located the wreck he made his way out to it where he found the pilot still alive but with the cockpit canopy jammed.

After struggling in vain to access the cockpit, he and his team were forced to withdraw from the scene by the rising tide. Upon returning to the site at low water the next day, the remains of the aircraft and pilot had been all but totally consumed by the soft sand. He stated that as a result of this the body of W/Off Pyka was not recovered.

W/off Pyka (left) in front of Blackburn Botha at 10 AOS Dumfries Photo Dumfries and Galloway aviation museum

Official Records (ORB's Cark Walney)

It is clear that we have conflicting versions of this tragic event and we must now look at how the incident was recorded in Walney's Operational Records book and also what details we can glean from the way it was recorded by RAF Cark.

From 10 AGS Walney we have two entries dealing with the crash, one from the station's Sick Quarters and one by the Station Commander. Walney's Sick Quarters staff operated the station ambulance and recovery/rescue team; this is their entry for the 9/11/44:

"A Martinet aircraft crashed in the estuary near Cark. The crash notification was received by flying control at 15:40 hours but the station Medical Officer was not informed by the Duty Pilot Officer until 16:21 hours. The ambulance was sent out forthwith, but the locality of the crash had been so casually defined that, after several hours of fruitless search the ambulance returned. The aircraft embedded in soft mud, gradually settled down and was covered by the rising tide. It was reported some days later that Admiralty divers had been forced to suspend operations. The body of W/Off Pyka was not recovered."

From the Station Commander 10 AGS the entry for 9th November 1944 reads, *"Weather – N/N Westerly wind gusty at times, visibility 20-30 miles, Fair with bright periods. Martinet HP270, the propeller and reduction gear lost in flight. Aircraft crashed in the sea just below low water mark. The pilot, W/Off Pyka was killed. Salvage operations eventually abandoned. Action to be taken on defective reduction gear planet wheel bearing".*

The only entry we have concerning the crash from the ORB of RAF Cark is one line which reads, *"10/11/44 Martinet aircraft from RAF Barrow crashed*

The Leven Estuary sands... deceptively beautiful but dangerous *near Ulverston Viaduct, pilot killed."*

To establish the actual facts surrounding this incident (as best we can), we need to examine each of the three accounts we have and set them against tidal records and ORB entries, thereby winnowing to a sufficient degree as to be sure that we are close to the truth.

Account No.1 tells us very little in any detail but does confirm the crash site as being close to Ulverston Railway viaduct. It also tells us that the wreck was not located till the following day and that divers were brought in to attempt to recover the body of W/Off Pyka but were unable to do so.

Account No.2 does give more detail with regard to the cause of the crash and tallies with official records in that the aircraft shed its propeller in flight. What cannot be correct in the way that this story found its way around 10 AGS after the event, is the idea that Pyka had escaped the crash only to drown or die in the sands. This part of the story is problematic as we know that a team of Admiralty divers toiled for at least three days before abandoning their efforts due to the wreck becoming submerged in the sand (10 AGS ORB entry). What does tally with account No.1 is the fact that C/PL Shirley remembered quite clearly that it was the day after the crash that the wreck was located.

We run into serious difficulties with account No.3 on many levels, the first being that had RAF Cark found the wreck straight away then there would have been no need for the extensive and fruitless search described in Walney's ORB. Secondly, the crash occurred late in the afternoon of a November day and by the time notification was received it would already have been growing dark. Tidal records tell us also, that high tide was at 18:41 hours on the evening of the 9th November 1944. The aircraft impacted below the low tide mark, as Walney's ORB tells us and so the tide would have been running very close to the time of the crash. It is a fact that when the ambulance team arrived in the area, having left Walney at 16:21 hours, the aircraft would probably have been completely submerged.

Low water next morning was at 01:37 hours, again during the hours of darkness and the first opportunity for a sighting of the aircraft would have been at afternoon low water which was at 13:54 hours. This confirms the suggestion that it was next day that the wreck was found, very likely as a result of an aerial search. The two questions begging answers are: If Cark's rescue team did make it to the wreck and were beaten back by the tide, why did they not inform RAF Walney's team that no further action or recovery was possible till the next day? Also, if the aircraft was upright and access to the cockpit possible, why then was extraction of the pilot not a fairly simple matter at low water the following day?

I think that the account W/Cdr Gibb gave of an attempted rescue offshore was probably not of this one and perhaps described another incident in which he was involved during his long career. We must bear in mind also, that the incident only rates a single one line entry in RAF Cark's ORB for the day and one would have expected more detail.

Construction of possible scenario

I must emphasise that the following offering is supposition only but has been constructed in the wake of discussion with several pilots, ex RAF airframe fitters and the Queen's guide to the Morecambe Bay Sands, Mr Cedric Robinson.

The Miles Martinet was powered by a Bristol Mercury radial engine which was encased in a substantial cowling. With the loss of the propeller of HP270, this cowling would have had a tremendous effect on the flying speed of the aircraft. Also, if further damage had occurred to the airframe due to fragmentation of the engines reduction gear casing, then the Martinet would have become very difficult to control.

W/Off Pyka is remembered as a determined and very skilled airman who would have fought his stricken aircraft to the very last and would most likely have chosen the flat sand for a belly landing, rather than water. It is possible then that he had so little control of the Martinet that no choice was available to him. With the propeller missing and with the gaping cowl to act as a water scoop, it is likely that the aircraft was thrown onto its back by the sudden deceleration. If this were indeed the case then it would explain the difficulty

Miles Martinet clearly showing broad engine cowling

in reaching the pilot's body, as the operation would involve cutting through the underside of the fuselage to do so.

Almost seventy years after this tragic event we will never know the true facts for sure and all views offered by myself are purely conjecture. What we can be certain of is that both W/Off Pyka and his aircraft remain under the sands of the estuary to this day, but can we say with any certainty, where?

During the course of my investigations into the crash of the Martinet I was given a location for the crash by no less than five local people and in all five cases the general area was the same. At a place almost halfway between Cark Airfield and the Ulverston Viaduct close to Sandgate Marsh is a point on the Ordinance Survey map marked as "Crook Wheel".

All five sources consulted agree that it is out on the sands opposite this location that the Martinet crashed. We know from official records that the aircraft went into water and I think it very likely that this water was the channel of the River Eea which runs into the sea there (see map).

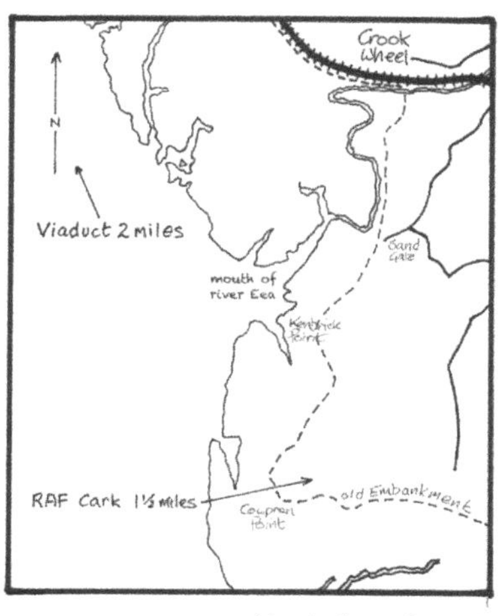

Map by Stuart Barnard

The running water in this area would quite likely render the sand very unstable and would account for the rapid sinking of the aircraft over a very short period of time. In the seventy years since this incident no-one has so much as glimpsed any part of the aircraft's remains and it is likely that the wreck currently lies under a possible 1½ to 2 metres of sand, a lonely grave for a brave man a long way from his homeland.

The final month of 1944 saw training course No.107 commence on the 2nd of December. An improvement in overall weather conditions enabled an almost full flying programme. Only one incident was to mar the month and it did not involve a Walney aircraft.

A Wellington arrives. 'A' Flight personnel (based on N/S runway) in foreground.

At 13.10hrs on the 18th of December, the unit's Medical Officer and ambulance team were called to a crash at Askam-in-Furness. Upon arrival at the scene they discovered the wreck of Martinet MS843, badly impacted into the soft ground and debris spread over a large area. The aircraft's pilot, P/O P Vose, of the Fleet Air Arm, had been killed instantly. No official cause for the crash could be established and we are left, once again, to perhaps conclude that an engine failure may have been the culprit. We do know for a fact that the Martinet did not shed its propeller in flight, as did W/O Pyka's aircraft, because in the early 1990s a JCB, whilst installing a gas or water main, dug up a propeller blade at the crash site.

December, 1944 was to see the start of the "Battle of the Bulge", the very last German Offensive and one that was to end in failure. The war in Europe was nearing its climax. In spite of this, training at RAF Walney continued at full capacity whenever weather conditions allowed and, with the new year, viewed with increasing optimism.

'A' Flight with Avro Anson LT777 (13).
L to R
7th from left (seated) Flt Lt Jim Reason, 7th from left (rear) LAC William Smith
WAAF row - 2nd from left Edith Owen, 6th from left Elsie Rhodes, 2nd left Ethel Cunningham

10 AGS personnel and 2 station officers pose outsideNo.1 hangar in front of Anson NK509

LACW Joan Metcalfe
LACW Elsie Rhodes
LACW Marion Jackson
LACW Marion Quiney

LACW Joan Metcalfe
LACW Elsie Rhodes
LACW Gloria Finley
LACW Marion Quiney

LACW Elsie Rhodes
LACW Greta Hogarth
LACW Joan Metcalfe

ACW Greta Hogarth
LACW Joan Metcalfe
LACW Ethel Cunningham

Ready for takeoff! Unidentified group in full flying kit - 10AGS

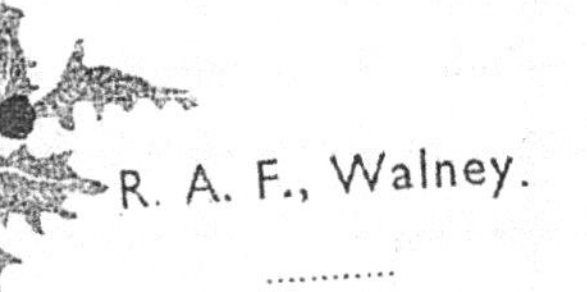

R. A. F., Walney.

Xmas Menu 1944.

Creme of Vegetable Soup.
Fried Fillets of Fish.
Roast Turkey.
Sage and Onion Stuffing.
Roast Fillet of Pork.
Roast Potatoes.
Creme Potatoes.
Brussel Sprouts.
Christmas Pudding.
Custard Sauce.
Beer.
Lemonade.
Biscuits and Cheese.
Apples.
Bread Rolls.

The Commanding Officer, Officers and Senior N.C.O.'s wish you all "A HAPPY CHRISTMAS."

Xmas menu courtesy of ex LACW Joan Metcalfe

Top right signature of Flt Lt C.Barrett ('C' Flight) who flew Martinets and Spitfires.
After the war he ran the King William hotel in Kirksanton and later flew as a private pilot from Walney.

CHAPTER SIX

1945
Spitfires Posted in to 10AGS

Flying at No.10 AGS commenced on the 2nd of January, 1945 at 9.20hrs and ceased at 16.40hrs, with no less than 132 flying details completed. The weather for the day was recorded as, *"Wind west-north-west 10-20mph, visibility 2-4 miles at first improving 8-10 miles. Cloudy, showers in the afternoon."*

It was during the latter part of the day when Anson LT741 took off from RAF Walney to rendezvous with a target towing aircraft over the sea and carry out a routine gunnery exercise. One can only assume that the pilot became disorientated after entering thick cloud and after straying for some time, took a westerly heading which he knew would take him away from the inland high ground and out to sea. Tragically, at an altitude of approximately 1,200 feet, the Anson crashed into the crags and screes of Eller Peatpot, on the flank of Black Combe.

It would be eight days later, on the 10th of January that the crashed aircraft was finally located by an Anson from RAF Cark, dropping flares to direct RAF Millom's Mountain Rescue team to the site of the accident. It was discovered that of the four man crew, three had died instantly from the initial impact and subsequent fire. One unspecified member had survived with a fractured right leg and minor burns, only to remove himself some distance from the blazing wreck and succumb to exposure. In this day and age it seems incredible that a crashed aircraft could remain undiscovered for so long. The fells, however, were not used for leisure then to the extent that they are today. The crew of LT741 were Flt/Sgt Pilot Wood, W/O Johnson, Sgt Turner (pupil gunner) and Sgt Jenkins (pupil gunner).

The unit was now very close to receiving its first deliveries of Wellington aircraft from various Maintenance Units. The Wellington had been more or less stood down from operational duties and many could be made available for training purposes. The type was perfect for air gunnery training as it carried gun turrets front and rear. It is obvious from an entry in station records for

hilippa Nixon shown here with one of the few remaining
agments of LT741and the aircraft's approx impact point.

Debris from LT741 still showing alloy manufacturers mark (ALCLAD)

John Nixon Jnr with undercarriage leg and wheel of LT741 Black Combe, Summer 1993. This artefact now held by Barrow Air Cadets in their HQ.

the 9th of January that the harsh environment of Walney was taking its toll on the poor old Ansons. N5062 was flown out to No.75 MU to be struck off charge due to, "severe deterioration of the aircraft due to weather conditions at Barrow."

It seems that at the outset of 1945, there was a large American Naval presence in the town. A reminder of the racial prejudice which existed in America during these years (and beyond), comes in the form of a bitter entry by RAF Walney's Senior Medical Officer on the 15th of the month. He writes, "AC2 Bobb Nursing Orderly admitted to Sick Quarters having been beaten up by Americans at a local dance. Group HQ contacted re advisability of posting a West Indian Negro to an American infested zone."

By the 27th of the month the weather had turned cold in the extreme, with all waterborne sanitation frozen solid. Elsan's (chemical toilets) were introduced, as the use of flush toilets was simply impossible and braziers were employed to keep the station's mains water supply functional. It was winter on Walney and everyone knew it!

On the 10th of February, 1945 the first two of the anticipated Vickers Wellington aircraft arrived to begin replacing the now tired Avro Ansons. These were MKX aircraft ferried in from No 48 MU at RAF Hawarden, near Chester. Not only did these aircraft possess two gun turrets, but being much larger than the Anson they could carry a larger number of pupils, leading to an increase in efficiency of the flying training details.

The number of Wellingtons on station strength increased throughout February and as it did so the unit's Ansons were steadily flown out. The heavier Wellingtons, however, began to cause wear and damage to the station's runways straight away, so repair and maintenance of them was made a priority.

On the 12th of March a Martinet aircraft was lost to the unit through yet another engine failure. HP308 piloted by P/O Ostrowski and with LAC Flanagan as his winch man, began to lose power to such a degree that a forced landing was necessary. This was just on the outskirts of Bootle, on the Cumberland coast; the stricken aircraft hitting overhead electric cables in the process. Fortunately, both men escaped with very minor injuries from an accident which could have so easily proven fatal.

Due to RAF Walney's geographical location, the airfield was saviour to many aircraft in difficulty and had been from the time of its opening. On the 16th of March a Hurricane KX878, on a ferry flight to No 22 MU, was forced to divert to RAF Walney due to a fuel shortage. Unfortunately, upon landing the aircraft nosed over, though with little damage caused to the machine. The

DUKW 'Seagull' used over 90 times during its 2 year service at Walney (though not all for aircraft crashes) WAAFs in front 3rd from left Freda Bell of North Scale, Walney. Middle row far right Italian POW, Tony.

station's Medical Officer rushed to the scene, but by the time he arrived at the aircraft there was no casualty. In fact the pilot wasn't there! The disgruntled M/O wrote in his log, "Having attended the crashed Hurricane of 16/3 it was obvious no injuries had been sustained as the pilot of the aircraft was already in the Officers' Mess by the time I arrived." (Editor - Nothing like a stiff drink after a prang, eh!)

As part of the station's air-sea rescue plan the unit operated a DUKW amphibious truck, as did RAF Millom. Of the acronym DUKW, 'D' represents a vehicle built in 1942, U is for 'Utility', 'K' means the vehicle was front wheel driven and 'W' is for two powered rear axles. Otherwise, the vehicle is affectionately known as 'Duck'.

On the 4th of April, a simulated sea rescue was carried out using the DUKW vehicle and all available flying personnel took part in the dinghy drill. The dinghy drill would likely be carried out in a body of static water on the airfield and I should imagine it was a very chilly experience for those concerned. Having said that, I'm sure that the drill did impress upon the participants the fact that you cannot always ditch at the right time of the year!

It is likely then that at least some of the crew of Wellington LP981 would have taken part in the training day of the 4th. On the 13th of April, the aircraft struck the sea off the Fylde coast with seven crewmen on board; five lost their lives. They were the pilot, W/O Trzebiatowski, an instructor and three trainee gunners (names not recorded). Two young trainee gunners were rescued by Fleetwood Lifeboat. They were LAC R Bembridge and LAC T Bedell. W/O Trzebiatowski is buried in Barrow Cemetery. No reason for the crash is recorded and no supposition is offered by station records - the cause remains a mystery.

By the end of April, 13 Ansons had left the unit and five more Wellingtons were flown in as replacements. Also arriving at the end of the month were six MKIIA Spitfires from No.7 SFTS (Service Flying Training School). These were to be the first of 26 such aircraft, of various early MKs, brought in to present fast, slippery targets for the trainee gunners. The Spitfires would not be towing a target, but would actually be the target for the pupil gunners who would be using camera guns, which would record their accuracy, or otherwise! The Martinets would continue to tow targets as they had always done, but this use of the old fighters would add another dimension to their training altogether.

Once at the vanguard of Britain's air defence earlier versions of the Spitfire, now tired old warhorses, found an equally important role at training units such as 10 AGS

It was May, Hitler was dead by his own hand and Soviet troops were entering Berlin, but at RAF Walney it was business as usual. An average of over 70 details a day was still being flown, though the numbers of pupils per course was beginning to fall.

The wreckage of Wellington LP891 on the Fleetwood sands.

Wreckage of LP891 showing tail section and rear turret.

However, all flying was cancelled on the 8th of May as VE Day was celebrated and an "all ranks" dance held that evening. I think it is a fair indication that a good time was had by all, in that only 21 details were flown the next day!

With this reduced average number of details being flown daily and the much improved weather conditions, it is perhaps no surprise that from this point on, the unit's accident rate fell in a dramatic way. Only one incident is recorded for May, when Wellington HZ272 hit the sand dunes on its landing approach, damaging its undercarriage which collapsed as the aircraft touched down (no injuries or names recorded).

The 1st of June saw RAF Walney's first Spitfire crash when P8248 suffered an undercarriage collapse on landing, due to the fracture of the hydraulic pump drive shaft. The pilot was uninjured (no name recorded). During the month, 15 Spitfires and a further six Wellingtons were flown in to the unit from various stations and RAF Walney continued to fly between 60 and 70 training details per day.

Only one further incident was to occur in June when Wellington LP925 having suffered a starboard engine failure, overshot during an emergency landing and burst into flames. Incredibly, the two crewmen managed to escape the burning wreck without injury (no crew names recorded).

Squadron Leader D.N. Forde, DFC flew in to RAF Walney on a preliminary visit on the 2nd of July. This was prior to him taking over command from Grp/Cpt Freestone later in the month.

On the 12th of July, a call was received from RAF Cark to report a forced landing by one of RAF Walney's Wellingtons out on the Morecambe Bay Sands, just off their airfield. The aircraft was NC780 which had attempted a single engine emergency landing at RAF Cark, following failure of the aircraft's port engine. This resulted in an overshoot by the crew (no crew names recorded).

Again, no crew names or aircraft number are recorded for the Martinet which was lost on the 19th of the month, nor any mention of injuries which may have been sustained by the crew. The aircraft crashed on take-off following yet another engine failure. It was to be followed by one more Martinet crash just five days later, the very last Martinet accident in the station's history and one which almost proved fatal.

The following is a transcription of RAF Walney's ORB entry of the 24th of July, beginning at 17.01hrs, *"A Martinet MKI (No HP279) had engine failure at 2,000ft, while flying over the sea. The pilot, Sgt Kreciala (Polish 704914), made a good landing in the sea about one minute after the failure. He ditched at*

Eskmeals. The plane sank in about 8 seconds. The Pilot carried no dinghy. Tow target operator's dinghy was washed away by the swell, having not been securely fastened to him he states. He stated he heard the Pilot speak in Polish over the RT but got no warning of the impending crash. Both men floated in their Mae Wests. The DUKW rescue vehicle left the station at 17.15hrs and made for the site of the crash guided by circling planes from this unit."

The next ORB entry was made at 18.45hrs and reads, *"DUKW reached scene of crash and rescued Sgt Kreciala, the pilot, who was unconscious, and suffering from shock and exposure, being pulseless, and not far from lifeless. He was taken back in the DUKW to Walney and admitted to station Sick Quarters there. The tow target operator (221873 F/Sgt Walker WG) was rescued about the same time*

Sea Otter

by a Sea Otter aircraft and flown to RAF Millom where he was admitted to their Sick Quarters, suffering from shock and immersion concussion."

As nothing to the contrary appears in the station's record book we must assume that both these men recovered from their ordeal, though the outcome of the incident would, without doubt, have been very different, but for the unit's swift response. The rest of July passed without mishap and S/Ldr Forde, DFC took command of the airfield on the 28th of the month.

August was to pass with little of import recorded in the unit's ORB. On the 15th of the month, the Japanese formally surrendered and the station celebrated VJ Day, though little of the festivities are mentioned in RAF Walney's records.

'A' Flight

Back row right Elise Rhodes

Wellington propellor change ('A' Flight)

Drogue packers - 10AGS

'A' Flight Vickers Wellington LP962
Groundcrew LACW Joan Metcalfe (flight mechanic airframe) seated on aircraft.

'A' Flight Vickers Wellington
Groundcrew LACW Marion Jackson & LACW Elsie Rhodes seated on aircraft.

On the morning of the 8th of September, 1945 Wellington XLP887 took off from RAF Walney. At her controls was W/O D.R. Jones and in addition to the two gunnery pupils, three young Air Cadets were also on board the flight. As W/O Jones flew the Wellington out to sea to begin firing practice on the ranges, the trainee gunner in the nose turret ejected a full belt of ammunition into the aircraft's propellers, badly damaging them. W/O Jones is recorded as making a textbook emergency landing with his damaged machine and it is further recorded that his flying log was endorsed for good airmanship. I wonder what he said to the pupil gunner when he landed!

The 15th of September, 1945 saw the station hold an "At home day". Attended by an estimated 10,000 members of the public, they were entertained by mock attacks on Wellington bombers by Spitfires and low level flypasts by a Lancaster, Anson, Oxford, Mosquito, Martinet, Master and a Typhoon which had flown in for the occasion from RAF Milfield. At the close of flying the Typhoon was found to be unserviceable, its Coffman starter having to be replaced before it could return to its unit that same evening. As a result, a total of £52/10s was raised for the RAF Benevolent fund, mostly in the form of donations as little in the way of refreshments was on offer at the occasion.

Although the war was now over and many RAF units were disbanding, with airfields being closed and "mothballed" under "Care and Maintenance" orders, RAF Walney by contrast had been earmarked for a service life beyond the close of hostilities. On the 29th of September, command of RAF Walney changed once more when Grp/Cpt HM Garnons-Williams arrived to formally take over, having been posted in from No.2 Flying Instructors School.

At the beginning of October down at RAF Woodvale, near Southport, No.577 Squadron received word that they were to transfer to RAF Walney. The C/O of this detachment, FltT/Lt Wrae, arrived at Barrow on the 4th of the month. The small unit arrived over three days on the 9th, 10th and 11th of October, bringing with them four Vultee Vengeance aircraft and two Spitfires. The RAF Walney detachment of 577 Squadron received only sporadic work and would rely on requests being made for aircraft to provide targets for radar calibration, or for drogue target towing in the many gun ranges which still operated along the Lancashire coastline.

Despite the fact that the war was now over, the station still held a substantial population, was flying an average of 40 details each day and had 130 gunnery cadets under training. Exact numerical statistics were:

RAF Officers	49
RAF Senior Ranks	84
RAF Other Ranks	289
RAF Cadets	130
WAAF Officers	4
WAAF S/NCOs	6
WAAF Other Ranks	171
Personnel Total	733

By December, however, the unit more and more resembled one which was winding down, as it began to steadily fly out its aircraft to various Maintenance Units across the country. Over the first week of the month alone, four Wellingtons, two Martinets and a Spitfire left the station for unrecorded destinations, the likelihood being that they were to be struck off charge and scrapped.

A further Spitfire was to be the last to join the unit on the 14th of December. Whilst on its way there the pilot of W3828 was forced to land his aircraft on the Morecambe Bay Sands, near RAF Cark, following an engine failure which was due to an obstruction in the machine's fuel line. RAF Walney's DUKW attended the scene, but discovered upon arrival that the pilot was unharmed and had made his way to shore to be given dry clothing and hot food by the staff at RAF Cark. I am told that the Flookburgh fishermen helped recover the wrecked Spitfire from the sands, though this is not officially recorded, nor is the pilot's name.

By the time RAF Millom ceased to operate in a flying capacity, the station had a very well established, efficient and active Mountain Rescue unit. This team was subsequently moved to RAF Cark. Now with the closure of RAF Cark imminent, the team was to be posted to and operate from RAF Walney, the move to take place in the early part of the January, 1946.

CHAPTER SEVEN

1946
Still Operational with the End Nigh

Christmas 1945 had come and gone with little of note of it in station records, however, the unit's first accident of the year occurred on the 4th of January. Spitfire EP651 crash landed at Firrie, near Penrith, after running out of fuel and the pilot (name not recorded) escaped with minor cuts and bruises. Yet another old Spitfire the MUs would not need to deal with!

RAF Cark's transferred Mountain Rescue team arrived at RAF Walney early on the morning of the 9th of January. They had only been in the station for a mere two hours when they were called to assist the unit's M/O following the demise of Wellington NC801 in the sand dunes on the airfield's perimeter.

Flying Control Operators 10 AGS
Back Row Jones, Sgt J.Thornton, Sgt Dransfield
Front Row W/O Gleed, W/O Kilsby, F/O Roach, FCO, Sgt Gibbs

The aircraft had suffered an engine failure upon landing, resulting in a catastrophic undershoot. We can assume that fatalities did not result from this accident as no fire was ignited in the crash and no crew names, or injuries to them, are recorded.

On the 3rd of February, the Mountain Rescue team received their first real call out from RAF Walney, following reports that a Dakota aircraft was believed to have crashed on, or near Skiddaw. After searching throughout that day, word was received that the crashed aircraft had been located by another search team from RAF Crosby, in Eden.

Yet another No.10 AGS pilot had an injury-free escape on the 12th of March. The undercarriage of Spitfire BL591 collapsed upon landing causing the aircraft to veer off the runway into soft ground and overturn, snapping the fuselage in the process. The name of the pilot is not recorded.

A further Spitfire was lost from station strength on the 9th of April, again due to an undercarriage failure following an emergency landing. This was

W/O Harry (Pranger) Bourne with AR323

AR323 taken up on an air test by W/O Harry (Pranger) Bourne. During this test elevator control was lost due to a pin falling out of the control column. With the elevator being inoperative the landing was a hard one causing the aircraft's undercarriage to collapse.

Instument & Electrical section 10 AGS - Spring 1946

The accident which befell Martinet HP315 on the 15th of April, however, was entirely due to pilot error (name not recorded). He retracted the aircraft's undercarriage whilst still on the ground! Whoops!

On the 12th of May, 1946 RAF Walney was again open to the public as the station held another "At Home Day" to raise funds for the RAF Benevolent Society. Many aircraft types were on display and the crowds were treated to a flying display by Vickers-Armstrongs's Chief Test Pilot, Geoffrey Quill, in a Spitfire. On this occasion a sum of £347 was raised for the charity, at what would be the beginning of the unit's 'swan song'.

During the first week of June, 1946 word was finally received officially that No.10 AGS was to disband at RAF Walney. They were to reform in the same role at RAF Valley on Anglesey, along with their Mountain Rescue team. On the 16th of the month a full inspection of the unit's aircraft was carried out in preparation for the move, and transfer of the first items of the station's equipment began within days. The station was not to close, however, without one final tragedy.

No. 10 AGS. 28th March 1946.
'C' Flight. Martinet and Spitfire Pilots.
Standing Left to right. Polish Air Force Pilots. W/O Maslanko, F/O Kazycki,
W/O Kubiak, Flt Sgt Kozlowski, Flt Sgt Weber, F/O Ostrowski and W/O Milosz.
Seated L To R. Polish Pilot W/O Wisnewski, then W/O Firth, W/O McFarlane,
Flt Lt Garwood DFC, Flt Lt Powell (Flt Commander), W/O Harry Bourne and W/O Norman Ellis, W/O Kilner.
Both W/O Maslanko and W/O Wisnewski flew with the German Air Force in the first World War.
One of them is wearing the Iron Cross under his battle dress.

Martinet and Spitfire pilots 10 AGS.
L to R W/O Norman Ellis, Flt Sgt Kozlowski, Flt Sgt Weber, F/O Pasieka

Martinet, Wellington and Spitfire Pilots.
L to R Flt Sgt Kozlowski, Flt Sgt Weber, Flt Sgt Weber (not related) and W/O Norman Ellis

Martinet, Wellington and Spitfire Pilots.
L to R W/O Dobson, W/O Norman Ellis, Flt Sgt Kozlowski, Flt Sgt Weber, W/O Cooke, W/O D.Oldham and Maitland (all Wellington pilots)

On the afternoon of the 1st of July, Wellington LP764 of RAF Walney transmitted an SOS call from out over the Irish Sea stating that the aircraft was to be ditched. At the controls was F/O Bob Gray and with him that day was F/Lt Flower of the Royal New Zealand Air Force. No reason for a landing on water is recorded, so we must assume that it was made necessary by engine problems.

Three versions of the reasons behind the flight of LP764 that day have been offered down the years. Firstly, that it had flown to Ireland to bring back beer for the station's closing down party. Secondly, that it was simply on an air test and finally, that the Wellington was loaded with surplus ammunition from RAF Walney, which they were to dispose of out at sea. Aircraft were dispatched to search for the two airmen, but to no avail. It would be some days before the body of F/O Gray was washed ashore near Silecroft and a further time before the body of F/Lt Flower was discovered much further north, near Port Patrick in Scotland. F/O Gray was only one week away from his demob and return to civilian life; he is buried in Walney Cemetery. F/Lt Flower is buried in Stranraer, a long way from his native New Zealand.

RAF Walney's final Gunnery Course

Back row 2nd from right - W/OP Ron Wood. Bottom right F/Eng Gordon Gill. The gentleman in civilian clothes I believe to be Group Captain Robinson (why he is not in uniform is unknown). To his right sits Flt Lt Flower.

Sgts Mess Staff 1946
Back row 1st left Sgt Wop/AG Des Tomlinson who went on to serve with 97 Squadron

Gordon Jenkinson with Auster Aircraft, Walney 1947
One of 3 Austers operated by Loxham Flying Services between Walney, Lancaster, Morecambe and Blackpool. The first civilian company to fly from the airfield.

By September, 1946 RAF Walney had all but fallen silent and by the beginning of December the airfield had been vacated but for a small division of Care and Maintenance staff. No.10 AGS was now fully operational, in post at RAF Valley.

The final RAF unit to operate from Walney (CO F/Lt Len Redshaw) arrived in October 1947. This was No.188 Gliding School for Air Cadets. The school flew Cadet MKI, MKII, MKIII gliders and later the Sedbergh TXI design. Records show that with the exception of a few months during the winter of 1947 -1948, the school used the airfield until the 1st of September, 1955 which marked the end of an RAF presence on Walney forever.

Over the years more than one attempt has been made to establish commercial aviation on the old airfield. None, however, have met with lasting success. Today the airfield is maintained and operated by BAE Systems, with a civilian gliding club flying from its runways at weekends.

With the outbreak of war, airfields began to appear very rapidly right across the British Isles. The greater numbers of these are forgotten, having been consumed by industrial estates, or have disappeared under farm land from where they had sprung.

Here in south Cumbria, our three wartime airfields have found post war lives for themselves. RAF Millom as HM Prison Haverigg and RAF Cark as a skydiving club operating their busy Islander Aircraft every weekend that our fickle coastal weather allows.

It is at Walney airfield, however, with its two well-maintained runways, control tower and hangar that one gets a strong feeling of an airfield patiently awaiting the return of its former occupants. If you still yourself and close your eyes, you can perhaps imagine that the steady engine drone above you is not the glider tug, but a Martinet towing its drogue target out to sea.

John Nixon

RAF Walney Island

10 Air Gunners School

Motto - We Prepare to Fight

1st December 1941 to 30th June 1946

SECTION TWO

Courses held at 10AGS

Nº 64 COURSE · WOP/AGs

SQUAD 1	SQUAD 2	SQUAD 3	SQUAD 4	SQUAD 5
HOGGARD · PEACOCK	BETTS · RUNYARD	HOGBEN · WARREN	WHITE · WAINWRIGHT	BREAREY · LYON
GOODALL · JENNINGS · SAXBY	COSTA · POCOCK · RAWSON	REEVE · OULD · CLARKE	ATKIN · HILL · WHEELER	BEARDS · JONAS · QUELCH
HALL · KEMPIN · SMITH	BOYLE · WHITEHALL · SNEYD	PERERA · LAYDEN · PATTERSON	BOOTHBY · WILCOX · AVEYARD	KERRISON · ANDERSON · HEWITT
URKE · SGT BUTTERISS (Inst) · AUSTIN	CLOVAN · SGT MARTIN (Inst) · BONES	BULLOCK · SGT MATTHEWS (Inst) · WALKER	WOOLDRIDGE · SGT MOSS (Inst) · JENNINGS	SYMONDS · SGT ROGERS (Inst) · SARGEANT
FEAVER · LEE	DYMOND · BURTON	WHYTE · NIMMO	EVANS · ARABIAN	KANO · HARRISON

In the first, and limited edition of this book we were fortunate to be able to include over 60 course photographs obtained from the National Archives. However due to copyright restrictions we had to restrict our limited edition print run to 199 copies. The course photograph you see here was provided by Mr David Lyon from Canada whose father trained at 10 AGS on Course No.64.

Courses would average around 40 pupils of all ranks from LAC to Sergeant and already qualified as Fitters engine/airframes. Work would begin in the classroom, with a great deal of theory, and in the ground based turret trainer on the moving target range, the latter to prepare them for the next airborne phase of their training.

SECTION THREE

No.128 Squadron Air Defence Corps, Barrow-in-Furness and its band.

No 128 Squadron Air Defence Cadet Corps, 1940/41.
Barrage balloon site No.7 Bella 111, Friars Lane, Barrow-in-Furness
– about 100 yards south of what was the Friars Hotel (now houses).
The ADCC cadets in full uniform and one in civvies.

L to R
Terry Lindsey, Stan Pearson, Les Wilkes, Wally Waddington (stood)
& six members of the Royal Air Force, Balloon Operators

Origins of The Air Training Corps

The British Air Defence Cadet Corps were founded by the air league of the British Empire in 1938. Not least of all due to the huge amount of interest being generated by aviation at that time. Initially 100 squadrons were formed with No.128 Squadron, Barrow-in-Furness being established in April 1939.

The headquarters for the squadron were initially the technical college in Abbey Road, the drill hall and laterally what is now the Custom House Restaurant, which had a rifle range alongside. Sponsorship for 100 uniforms was provided by Sir Charles Craven and Sir John Fisher.

The Air Defence Cadet Corps became The Air Training Corps in April 1941, at which time Mr Peter Yuile (who provided us with these photographs) joined 128 squadron.

It was at this time that the uniform for Air Cadets changed, these photographs show cadets in Air Defence Cadet Corps uniform.

In the following pages, thanks to the photo archive of Peter Yuile, we see illustrated the operational lives of Colin Peters and Wally Waddington following their subsequent posting into the ranks of the RAF.

No 128 Squadron Air Defence Cadet Corps, 1940/41 'A' Flight.
Stan Pearson (or Les Wilkes), Terry Lindsey, Wally Waddington, & Colin Peters

ATC Cadets leave Avro Anson after air experience flight 10 AGS (date unknown)
(Ted Cowperthwaite in doorway)

A change of uniform, basic training, Blackpool December 1942.
AC2 ACH U/T WOP/AG Wally Waddington and AC2 ACH U/T Pilot Colin Peters.

Colin Peters

A Barrow lad born and bred. Colin spent his young life in New St, Barrow-in-Furness with his grandmother Mrs Woods. It is understood that his Uncle, George Woods, was licensee of the Robin Hood public house in Crellin St, Barrow.

After the war, Colin extended his service with the RAF. On the 24th August 1948 whilst flying Hawker Tempest NX209 with No 249 squadron based at RAF Habbaniya in Iraq he crashed 14 miles SE of the airfield and sadly died in hospital as a result of his injuries.

Flt Sgt Pilot Colin Peters No 33 squadron, shown here on the continent in early 1945. Colin was shot down by flak on 23rd April 1945 whilst flying Hawker Tempest SN173. After a forced landing 8 miles south west of Schleswig, North Germany - he spent 3 weeks as a POW.

Following his liberation from the German prisoner-of-war camp Flt/Sgt Colin Peters rejoined No.33 Squadron. This photograph shows him with a German Siebel SI204 on a Luftwaffe airfield at Dedelstorf North Germany in the Summer of 1945. The Siebel SI204 was a Luftwaffe navigation training aircraft which was also used for light transport duties.

Summer 1945, on Luftwaffe airfield Dedelstorf with Focke-Wulf 190A-4.

A tired looking aircraft surprisingly carrying some American markings (possibly test-flown and appraised by the allies following its capture or perhaps carrying the American Star to help it infiltrate allied bomber streams).

Following a spell at RAF Millom (1943-1944) as a staff wireless operator
Flt Sgt WOP/AG Wally Waddington with other crew members of the Halifax B111. LW646 MP-E
ofNo.76 Squadron. Holme-on-Spalding Moor.
Standing left to right:
F/O Douglas Bennett, Flt Sgt Gordon Purchase, Flt Sgt Jack Espie RAAF, Sgt Horace Wright (Lefty1),
Flt Sgt Wally Waddington. Kneeling L to R: Sgt Joseph Salt (Lefty2), Sgt Leslie Carrol (Spanner), Dog.

No 128 Squadron Air Defence Corps Band

No 128 ATC had formed a very accomplished band by 1943. Lead by W/O Archie Goodall (including Drum Major Andy Donaldson who joined the RAF in 1943 as aircrew, small chap to his left is Reg Denny). The band won several prizes for deportment and musical ability including a major event at Belle Vue in Manchester. They are seen here marching through Barrow-in-Furness and at a local show.

Battle of Britain Day

Full parade 128 Squadron ATC and their band, RAF Walney 12th September 1943 Battle of Britain Day. Cadets march past led by F/O Adam Denny. Taking the salute at the march-past was Major General S.B. Pope CBDSO the district inspecting officer. Somewhere amongst these ranks would be a young Peter Yulie.

128 Squadron ATC band in front of Vickers Wellington NC827. Photograph taken in the Spring of 1945. The band played at many parades, concerts and at the Squadron's dance held in the John Whinnerah Institute (on the corner of Abbey Rd & Hindpool Rd in Barrow-in-Furness) on the occasion of the band's first anniversary in May 1944

Front row: Tom Newton ATC, Cadet Roberts, W/O Archie Goodall (bandmaster), Flt/Lt Adam Denny, Flt/Lt Sid Hampshire, Flt/Lt Atkinson Johnny Rhodes ATC (drum major)
Middle row: Ken Martin, Bill Cubin, Glyn Jones, Frank Williams, Gordon Jenkinson, Reg Denny

128 Squadron ATC band parade 10 AGS 1946

SECTION FOUR

Aerial mementoes from 1947

We cannot be certain why these photographs were taken or from what type of aircraft. We do, however, know the time and date at which they were taken.

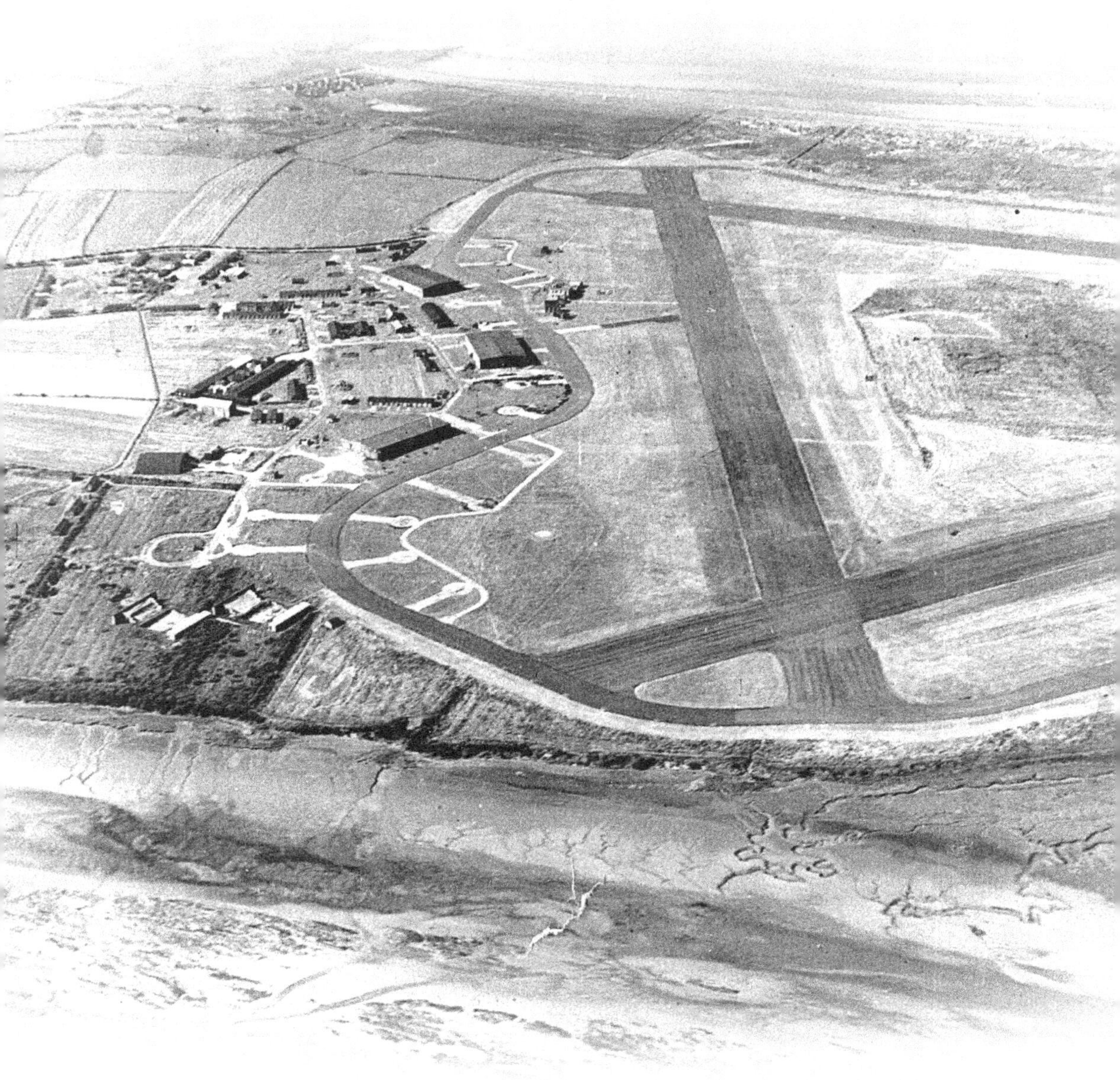

Aircraft departed, airfield closed 20th Aug 1947 10:30

Jubilee bridge over Walney Channel, Barrow-in-Furness
Photograph taken 10:30 on Wednesday 20th August 1947

No problems parking in Barrow-in-Furness in 1947. Not a car in sight! The wartime YMCA forces canteen is the building by the side of the park and the promenade.

Ulverston Cumbria, between Coast Road and Priory point.
Photograph taken 11:00 on Wednesday 20th August 1947

The shadow of the aeroplane can clearly be seen on the landscape. The buildings adjacent to this were the engine testing sheds used by Armstrong Siddely during the war for testing reconditioned Cheetah engines. The three airfields in the area (Walney, Cark & Millom) all operated Avro Anson aircraft powered by twin Cheetahs, which generated a great demand for these engines. After the war the disused plant was converted to grass-drying and then soap powder manufacturing. The site is now occupied by Kingfisher Building Products Ltd.

Canal Foot – South Ulverston, Cumbria.
Photograph taken 11:40 on Wednesday 20th August 1947

The photograph here shows a beautifully defined Canal Foot including end basin and lock gates. With netted swimming enclosure clearly visible at bottom right. Close examination will also reveal at the top of the picture Ulverston iron works with its rail line leading to the head of the slag banks. A landscape much changed today with the arrival of the Glaxo pharmaceutical manufacturing plant.

SECTION FIVE

Memories of RAF Walney

Having concluded a précis of the history of RAF Walney in so much as it was officially recorded, it is time now to move on to the personal accounts, anecdotes and recollections contributed by those who served there during the station's wartime life. When I first began my research I was curious about the background of the overseas trainees who arrived at RAF Walney, RAF Cark, RAF Millom and units like it. What drove these men and women who came across the globe to take up the fight against the axis powers? What sort of characters were they? And what course did their lives take on return to their home countries?

Alfred Wise Dudley - The Uniform Years 1940 - 1946

Prologue to my attempt to produce some sort of record of my wartime years, this, some 65 years after the actual events took place, but with, hopefully, enough memory recall left to establish a reasonably accurate chronicle of my life in uniform; "The Uniform Years".

I write this in somewhat unusual circumstances. As this is December 26th 2005, and finds me on holiday in Fuerteventura enjoying a very unusual Christmas and New Year. Quite unlike any I have experienced before, with warm sunny days. Although I have no doubt that by the time I get around to finishing this I will be back in the U.K. with the usual mix of long, dark, wet, cold days.

Strictly speaking, I suppose with regard to the wearing of uniform I should start with my Home Guard time or Local Defence Volunteers (L.D.V.) as it was first known. This was formed post Dunkirk, in May 1940, and open to everyone to volunteer above the age of 17. A bit of a "bits and pieces" arrangement to start with, but did become more professional as time went on with the issue of uniforms and rifles, and now looking like a sort of army. Not, I think, that it would have been much of a match for any invading forces dropping out of the sky, with a maximum of 5 rounds of ammunition available per man. We had our share of "Dads Army" characters too, they were all there. If it hadn't been about such a serious business, it would have been a laugh a minute, however, I suppose it did achieve a degree of propaganda and confused the enemies thinking, it certainly confused a lot of people here!

The really serious uniform time started rather later, and my first attempt to be of assistance in the conflict was early August 1940, a week after my 18th birthday. I made my way to the joint recruiting office in Manchester to volunteer for flying duties, but after a couple of interviews and some form filling, I was informed that I could not be accepted for aircrew training, as my educational qualifications were not of the required high standard (I had of course left school at the age of 14). However, I was told I could join the R.A.F as a general duties entrant, this offer I rejected and said I would go next door and join the Navy, not that I had any intention of doing this, there was too much cold water involved there!

However, my next attempt in April 1941 did meet with rather more success, as the reality of the situation had finally become recognised, in as much as losses in personnel were overtaking new entrants coming in, and the strict educational requirements were having to be relaxed to further a push for higher numbers to be brought into the system.

Dudley's heart murmur was not detected

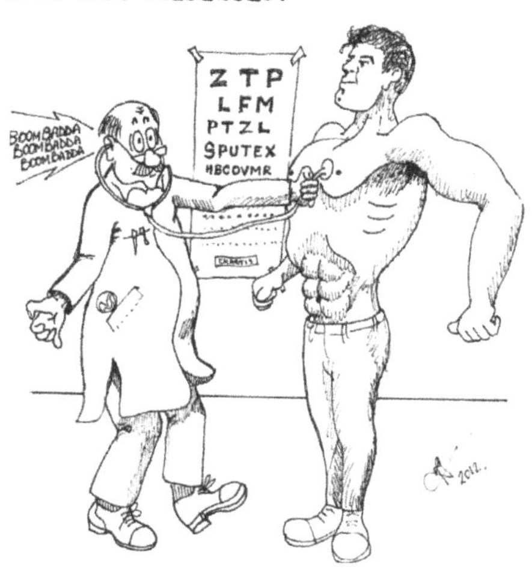

The powers that be, therefore, agreed that I could be finally accepted for aircrew training, and could be actually allowed to get into one of their aeroplanes! So it was off to Padgate for the aircrew selection board and medicals.

The medical examination was giving me some cause for concern at this time, as I had rheumatic fever as a child and was aware that I had a heart murmur as is usual post this illness. I also knew that this would have precluded me from aircrew duties, so I omitted to mention this on the form I was given to complete listing childhood illnesses and hoped for the best. Fortunately, a lot of the doctors who were doing the medicals were older retired practitioners who had been brought in to fill the gaps, and were not over efficient. The sheer numbers going through meant that things were a little rushed. My murmur was not picked up, even after the preliminary checks of blowing up a column of mercury and holding it for one minute and the quick whizz round in a chair and then standing on one leg, and various other things to be completed pre-medical.

More interviews followed, the whole process taking two full days, and then, I was finally accepted as a trainee WOP/AG (wireless operator/machine gunner), sworn in, accepted the "Kings Shilling", and then designated the service number 1049069. From that point on I was indeed just a number.

After this it was back to my civilian status and also the Home Guard on deferred service to wait until my number came up in the queue for places in the training schools. This finally arrived on September 19th 1941, and it was off to Padgate again for kitting out and then to Blackpool for the start of training proper.

RAF Squires Gate

I spent 4 months at Blackpool doing all the usual training stuff, drills etc. plus a round of inoculations, anti typhoid, typhus, malaria etc. all in anticipation of overseas postings. Pretty vicious stuff it was too. Knocked me out for nearly a week and for a couple of days I didn't know whether my arm belonged to me or not. These all to be topped up at a later date; I made a mental note of avoiding the next time, thinking there had to be a way of giving it all a miss. But more of that later. The main focus of the training was on learning and using Morse code. This was relentless and aimed at getting up to speed by a certain time. There were various venues for this, the best of which was the Winter Gardens and the worst was the disused Tram sheds (which was where I unfortunately was allocated to). They were cold, flag floors wth no heating. As the weather got colder, it necessitated the wearing of overcoats and gloves. We sat on long tables with a pair of earphones clamped on over a cap, for two 2 hour sessions every

day, and occasionally three. Really it was mass learning by saturation. With a test every 2 weeks and the speed being increased up to a maximum of 12 words per minute for passing out, there was only one second chance for a failed test. If failed again, it was a case of cease training – commonly known as CXd. Understandably this pressure of continuous Morse in the headset did affect a few people and resulted in a degree of temporary insanity. With 3 or 4 weeks in a psychiatric unit (Feldmans Arcade had been adapted for this purpose) they recovered quite quickly but were never allowed to return to the business of "Morse" in any shape or form.

Training apart, the things that most remain in my mind about Blackpool were, on the plus side, the wonderful efficiency of bath parades. These were twice a week at Derby Baths (long gone now of course) with thousands going through every day. If the shower was taken quickly, there was time for a few lengths in the main pool. It was all timed extremely well, with my squad allocated 5.15pm every Tuesday and Friday. The local hospitality was much in evidence too, and I remember particularly the cheap rides on the sea front trams. This was a maximum of one penny if in uniform, regardless of the distance travelled, and one could ride from Squires Gate to Fleetwood for this.

On the downside was my billet, it must have been one of the worst in Blackpool. Twenty eight of us in there, the food was awful, never properly cooked, and for example the same pudding every day of the week, and only a change on Sunday when it was rice. The landlady employed 3 or 4 young Jewish girls (refugees) and paid them a pittance. She was regularly seen going out by taxi in the evenings dripping in gold jewellery. There was a resident Corporal, who we had to address complaints to, but it didn't make any difference. I have always believed that he was getting a good pay off every week. Most of those Blackpool Landladies did a really good job and treated twi-SR boarders like their own sons, but for just a few it was an opportunity to make a lot more money than they had ever been able to make running second rate boarding houses. Afterwards I lived on many camps where cooking was on a mass produced scale, but never any as bad as my Blackpool experience. At least I was never hungry again, and didn't have to spend every penny I could spare on buying food!

Now, after acquiring the necessary speed of taking Morse, it was time to move on. After a weeks leave, it was off down to Yatesbury in Wiltshire, this being January 1942.

RAF Yatesbury

A cold bleak January it was, and turned into a long winter, continuously frozen up everywhere, and lasting until mid March. Not much heating in the huts or in the cookhouse which was a large Spartan building, with seating for up to a thousand. By the time the food had been collected and taken to the table there wasn't a lot of warmth left in it! However, one got used to the conditions eventually, and, as well as the continuation of the process of gradually increasing Morse speeds, there were now classroom and workshop periods we learned about the technical side of radio, fault finding experience mostly, to be able to decide which valve/fuse to change if the equipment went down whilst airborne. We also had some responsibility for the general electrical systems of the aircraft.

Before I move on from the Yatesbury period, there are a couple of incidents worth mentioning. One of which is the weekly sports afternoon, when everyone was expected to participate. It was football or rugby for many, as there were a dozen or so pitches available. As I wasn't any good at either of these, I found myself (along with a thousand or so others) taking part in a cross country run. Now, if it had been nice summer weather this would have been tolerable, but it was mid-winter and the ground was frozen solid (clad only in a T-shirt, shorts and a pair of thin plimsolls, it really wasn't much fun). I remember seeing a string of racehorses being exercised as we ran over the frozen ground. Alright for them though, they were covered in heavy blankets, and I thought there must be a better way of spending Wednesday afternoons than this. Sure enough the opportunity arose with a notice appearing on the notice board announcing the start of evening fencing classes, one night a week for 2 hours. I thought that enrolling for these might just be a good investment. With not many willing to give up an evening, so it proved to be. When the next sports day arrived I found myself excused to attend further fencing classes. I never actually made much progress with the fencing apart from learning how to put on the equipment, and the difference between a Foil, an Epee, and a Sabre, yet as it all took place in a nice warm hut it took care of my sports afternoons; there was always a way to beat the system!

The other small episode that might be worth mentioning concerns the next round of vaccinations. I didn't much fancy these, so after observing the procedure and knowing my day I prepared myself by a visit to the NAAFI store to buy a packet of plasters. Armed with these I went down to the medical hut and joined the queue waiting for injections. I rolled up my sleeve and stuck a plaster on my arm. I then joined the queue waiting to have pay books stamped to confirm injections given and displayed my bit of plaster. Result (pay book stamped and all quite painless, with no after affects at all!). As I mentioned before, there was always a way.

My time at Yatesbury finally ended in April 1942, and after the end of term exams, I was finally a fully trained radio operator. Plus I was in receipt of a 50% rise in pay, still not great but welcome nevertheless, it was actually from 3 shillings per day to 4 shillings and 6 pence. (In the metric scale this would be from 15p a day to 22p a day, difficult to make comparisons due to much changed values). Finally, it was home leave for a week and then on my way to No.10 Air Gunnery School as a staff radio operator, ground service.

RAF Walney

When I was first informed that my posting was to Walney Island I thought that I was going overseas as I had never heard of it. I suppose it was overseas in a way, being an island, but I was relieved to discover it only a short bus ride across the estuary from Barrow-in-Furness. The channel was up to the shipyards on the Barrow side, where the submarines being made were launched. I often stood on the bridge and watched, and wondered how many of their crews would survive the war. I remained at Walney for most of the summer of 1942, not leaving until mid-August. This proved to be a very enjoyable period as, being a radio operator and working shifts, I was excused all other duties and parades. I lived in a hut designated as a signals hut, with all the other signals operators – it was all very comfortable. We worked 12 hour shifts, alternate weeks on days and nights, with very little in the way of radio traffic. We were required to listen to Group Control broadcasts every hour, with an occasional individual message to 10 AGS (not that these were very important). I think it was just to make sure we were still awake! The whole network, with control at Preston, covered all the west coast, and was in place as a back-up in case of landlines being destroyed by enemy action. We had one day off a week and, as it was a particularly good summer, I made a habit of getting up mid-afternoon when on nights and going down to the beach for a couple of hours with a book, returning in time for an evening meal before going on 'watch' (the hours were 8 to 8). Sadly, as all good things must, it came to an end, and I found myself on my way down to London.

No.7 Signals School.

I arrived in London, South Kensington SW7, in mid-August 1942. The whole school were billeted in a block of flats, known as Albert Court Flats, directly opposite the Albert Hall. They had been and indeed still are, "Luxury Flats". All fittings had been stripped out of course, apart from essentials, and the lifts no longer worked. Not a lot of fun when living on the 6th Floor as I was, with 2 flights of stairs to each floor. It was very up-market after living in a hut, I think nearly everyone was surprised to find baths fitted with glass doors. Some more so than others, having probably never seen a bathroom before. There were a dozen or so of us to each flat.

The course was 14 weeks duration and designated as a Radio Maintenance Course. I only discovered in recent years that after passing out I had become "*Aircraftman 1st class Radio Operator Mechanic*". I don't remember ever noticing the increase in pay that should have gone with this sudden elevation in rank – wouldn't have been much though! Our classrooms were in the science museum, which had been stripped of all its contents for safe keeping until after the war's end. Workshops were in what had been the sculpture galleries and our dining room was in the basement of the arts building. A bit of a doubtful place this for a dining area, as I remember when on one occasion a drowned rat was discovered at the bottom of one of the large tea urns, (kind of puts you off tea!). We paraded daily on Cromwell Road before going off to classes. P.T. was in Hyde Park, quite pleasant this though. In the early days when the weather was still warm, a swim in the Serpentine was the order of the day, and when the weather was inclement, P.T. periods were in the Albert Hall. Suppose I can always claim to have appeared there.

As we were now in an advanced stage of training we did not have to be back in Barracks until 23.59hrs each evening – a privilege this for a training school, it was usually 22.30hrs. I was not the least familiar with the way around London, but soon found the tube system made it possible to quickly find the way to anywhere. With very little spare cash, it was not possible to sample many of the attractions that were still available, but I did manage a visit to St. Paul's Cathedral and to Kew Gardens, plus an occasional walk along the embankment and a few visits to speakers corner. I also remember what was probably the best forces canteen I ever encountered. It was in the basement of the Brompton Oratory, and staffed by the ladies of the church. Food and drinks were excellent with occasional cream cakes on the menu. (How did they do it?) Mid January 1943 brought an end to my stay in the capital.It was a pleasurable enough period and now I found myself on the way to Madley in Herefordshire, to at last be introduced to a real aeroplane!

RAF Madley

Madley did not appear to be very hospitable on arrival. It was a wartime built establishment, hurriedly put together. Nissan Huts and everywhere widely dispersed; each section seemed to be at least half a mile apart, with a long walk to the ablution site. After the long walk for a wash, it was a further long hike to the dining hall and classrooms, with a final stretch down to the flights. never being anywhere near the point of residence again all day, and it was essential to carry small kit around all the time i.e. shave and wash gear, and eating utensils. However, the course was quite enjoyable, and mainly aimed at using the radio equipment whilst airborne. This was at first in Dominies, a twin engine aircraft that was really quite small, but with enough space for 5 pupils and an instructor plus pilot – virtually a flying classroom (which worked very well).

The last 2 weeks were spent going solo in a single engine aircraft, Proctors, with just a pilot and then doing individual work on the radio. I found the whole process very pleasant, particularly so as flying was a completely new experience, as indeed it was for most of us. I really enjoyed flying up and down the Wye Valley. This all came to an end in early March 1943, and I was on my way to gunnery school for a course in air gunnery.

RAF Mona

So now I was off to Mona in Anglesey to No.3 AGS. Again this was a somewhat dispersed establishment, with Nissan Huts for accommodation. They were very cold at that time of year, with just a shelf running down each side of the hut. Very active those shelves were too at night, with mice running up and down.

Air Gunnery practice was done from Blackburn Bothas – not a very comfortable aircraft and extremely unpopular with most aircrew. Three pupils for each aircraft were carried, with 2 machine guns in the turret to fire 200 rounds each. We fired at a drogue towed by another aircraft, the tips of the bullets were coloured in order to establish which pupil was responsible for each hole in the drogue. They were then dropped in the dropping field, where they were then collected by WAAFs and the holes duly counted. I sometimes think they would add a few more hits to the score if they thought someone had a poor score. I never heard of anyone actually failing the course! In my end of term report I see that I was assessed as above average, I think some kind WAAF must have added a few to my total.

When firing was completed, some of the pilots would fly up to Blackpool to go round the tower a couple of times. One other incident occurred after a couple of weeks when we had started with the flying side of the course. I got my flying boots off the shelf in the hut, and a dozen or so little pink mice dropped out of them. It appeared that Mr. And Mrs. Mouse had set up home there, not much fur left on the boot! So it was off down to stores to exchange them for new pair – did me a good turn actually as the ones I got were a much better style and quality than the ones I was discarding.

My time at Mona came to an end in late March 1943. With passing out this time came promotion to the somewhat exalted rank of Sergeant, and with this came a very welcome increase in pay. It's difficult to quantify in terms of today's wages, but it more or less doubled my income. With the passing out parade came the list of postings to say where I was headed off to after a week's leave I found myself due to report to RAF Cark, No.1 SPTU. I had no idea at the time what sort of establishment it was, or indeed where it was but I was soon to find out!

RAF Cark

I soon found out RAF Cark was based in Flookburgh, close to Grange-over-Sands. That set the location, but I was still in the dark as to knowing what it was. It turned out to be another course, they seemed never ending – now to turn me into a Radio Instructor, Air Operating. It all sounded very grand and I could not imagine why I found myself earmarked for this. I can only think, in retrospect that my number had just been pulled out of a hat somewhere; I'm sure it wasn't due to any special ability on my part.

This six week spell proved to be very enjoyable as it was now late spring, with a lot of fair weather periods. Not much of the time was spent in classrooms, mostly it was spent airborne without an instructor. It was really just a case of working through the syllabus whilst flying on cross country exercises. We had a second pilot, one flying whilst the other did the navigating. They were training to be navigational instructors, to fly trainee navigators around, hence the name, "Staff Pilot Training Unit". My course work consisted mainly of supplying these trainee Pilot/Navigators with enough in the way of Fixes and Bearings to enable them to plot their course.

The aircraft in use were Ansons, in which I was to spend a lot of my time during the ensuing 18 months. I found them very comfortable if a little overcrowded with 5 crew members. Nothing exceptional occurred whilst at Cark. The only thing of note that I remember was flying in formation over Carnforth one Saturday afternoon, where they were having a "Fund raising day" for the war effort.

RAF Millom

On completion of the course I found myself on my way to Millom, designated No.2 AFU (Advanced Flying Unit) where the pupils were already qualified aircrew and were there to gain further air experience.

Millom seemed to be agreeable and friendly enough on my arrival. I found my quarters were to be a single room contained in a block, very small and sparsely furnished but nevertheless a pleasant change from living in a barrack block. It contained a bed, a small but comfortable enough chair and a small table covered with a piece of old blanket. There were no facilities for hanging clothes up, but a couple of nails in the wall took care of that. Heating consisted of just a single pipe running through the room, and I noted that there would be just enough space to park my cycle. The communal ablutions were situated at one end of the block, all very nice though, particularly so as this was the first time in my life that I had a room of my own! (I was now 20 years of age.)

On checking out the routines, I found out that the mess was only a hundred yards away and Millom itself about 3 miles distance. Hence the bike was to prove very useful over the following 18 months. A private laundry service was provided through the mess, paid for through a mess bill at the end of each month. Apart from clothing, sheets were changed weekly (as aircrew an extra privilege was to always have sheets), the mess was always able to come up with extra rations such as eggs and poultry (much of it I suspect obtained via the black market and the farms of the Lake District). Meal times were somewhat changed, with the main meal of the day now being evening dinner. This was to accommodate ever changing flight times, all of which was to maximise air time at 24 hours a day weather permitting. A light meal was served at lunchtime, with afternoon tea with sandwiches available in the anteroom for those who required them at about 4pm. We enjoyed waitress service for evening dinner. All-in-all it really was very civilised.

The downside to all this, of course, was having to be available to fly at any time of the day or night when the weather was deemed suitable. We flew in some fairly dodgy conditions and, as Ansons were not equipped with any de-icing facilities, plus the fact that they had a ceiling of about 12,000 feet, and could not often fly above the clouds, meaning that on frosty nights we were briefed to take care when approaching high ground!

On an organisational level we were divided into 4 flights; 2 flights on days and 2 on nights. We flew alternate fortnights days and nights, with one day off each week. Days off were usually spent in Barrow, with evenings in Millom when not scheduled to fly. The local pubs were the favourite venues. (Not much else to do in Millom). There was always the option of an early return to the mess when the pumps ran dry, as frequently happened in those days. Home leave came quite frequently; being aircrew we were allowed one week off in every six, normally taken as a fortnight every 3 months.

However, we did not suffer anywhere near the casualty rates of Bomber Command, where life expectancy for a new crew at this time was 5 operational flights. We did however suffer occasional accidents, with the limited capabilities of the aircraft – many of which had been well used before arriving at Millom. This, coupled with the fact that servicing was somewhat minimal, did lead to some problems. It has to be said though that most accidents with fatalities occurred due to weather conditions or errors in navigation. Mountains or high ground did have a nasty habit of getting in the way! We lost about a dozen aircraft with crews during my time there, plus many other accidents of a lesser degree – not that we were any different to other air training establishments. There were crashes of one sort or another every day. Over 100 aircraft perished on the slopes of Snowdon during those years. Four of our Ansons during my period found their graveyard there.

All of this apart, I really quite enjoyed my time there. Between Walney, Cark, and Millom I spent about half of my service life in that SW corner of the Lake District. It is only in retrospect that I perceive many of the delights there were in spending time in that neck of the woods. One that I particularly remember is of returning from the west after night details just as dawn was breaking on summer mornings, and flying into the rising sun, and seeing from the observation dome the mountains casting their first shadows, with the sun's rays reflecting from the lakes. Not that this was seen as anything special at the time, all we were thinking about then was getting back to egg, chips, and often bacon. Also, that would be served between night details; and if on the final flight, hoping that the next night's flying would be cancelled so that a visit to town could be arranged!

One other duty that should have been appreciated but wasn't, occurred only occasionally (twice in my case) involved changing the batteries on

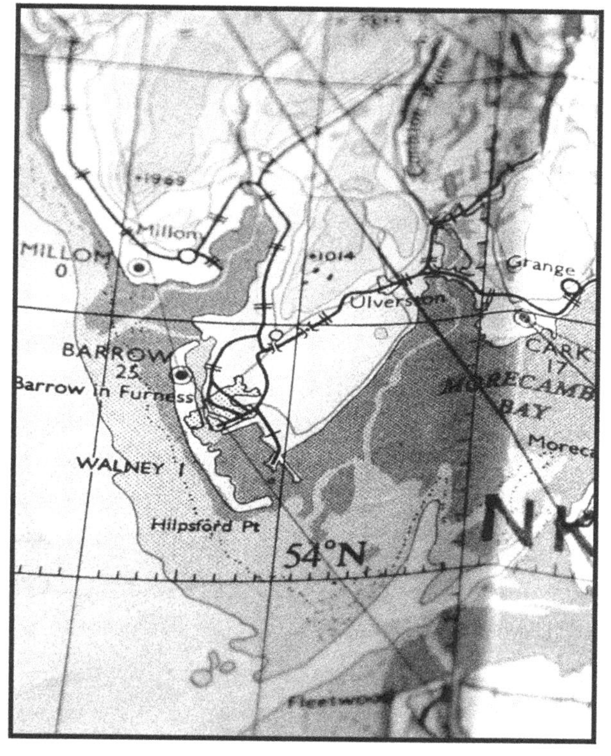

the mountain warning transmitters that were situated on high ground. These were heavy duty car type batteries carried in back packs designed for the purpose (certainly heavy!). We were in teams of 6 and took turns in carrying them, the whole process in getting to the top and back down again took about 5 or 6 hours. I remember on one occasion having to use ice picks to gain access to the container housing the equipment. When the changing process had been completed the discharged batteries had to be carried back down the mountain side. I suppose I can always claim to have climbed Scafell and Skiddaw, not so much of a climb really, as we were guided up the easy route by a local guide, it was heavy going though; there was however a bonus at the end of the day in the form of a evening meal laid on at a local hostelry, on one occasion this was the Royal Oak, Ambleside.

I was fortunate during my time at Millom not to have been involved in any accidents of any description, even minor ones. I did avoid (if that is the right word) 2 accidents that led to fatalities, simply because fate decreed that I was not in the wrong place at the wrong time. The first of these occurred in my early time there before we had become established with regular crews. One of my group asked me if I would mind changing with him because he had become friendly with a particular pilot, I agreed and on their first flight together the aircraft started to vibrate and finally broke up over St.Bees Head – they were all killed. The second occasion was on a weekend leave taken to be best man at a friend's wedding. When I returned from leave on the Sunday evening, I discovered that the crew that I would have been flying with (had I not been on leave) had crashed in Northern Ireland, with 2 crew members killed and the others in hospital. Thus it would appear that the gods were being extremely kind to me.

Two other small items that just might be worth mentioning – rather amusing both of them. The mess adopted a young jackdaw that had an injured wing and had difficulty flying. It quickly became at home in the dining room due to the scraps of food readily available, and also developed a taste for beer. It would perch on the glasses on the bar and drink from them, as you may well imagine this behaviour was much encouraged. The problems started when it was introduced to whisky and had great difficulty standing on one leg after a few drops of the short stuff and immediately fell over. This led to much hilarity all round. Afterwards it settled in a corner of an armchair, sleeping off the effects before waking up with an obvious hangover – with feathers on it's head standing to attention! Sadly it only survived for about 6 months, being so slow on the wing I can only imagine that some predator had a bit of a feast.

"IF YOU LET ME GO I COULD 'HOWT G'NAGIVATE THE LOT OF YOU!" HIC!

The other small detail that may be of some interest concerns the toilet facilities on the Ansons. As the aircraft was comparatively small there was no elsan available, just a funnel with a tube leading out into the slipstream for emptying one's bladder. Bit crude this, I often wondered about what some honest citizen passing underneath must have thought – probably, "that's funny, I didn't think it would rain today".

My time at Millom came to a sudden end, as all good periods must, when I returned from Christmas leave in 1944 to discover that all flying had ceased. There no longer being the need for more and more crews, quite suddenly there were more trained aircrew available than required. The war in Europe was moving towards closure and consequently demands were diminishing. So I, along with all the other flying personnel, found ourselves on the move again. I had enjoyed a comparatively comfortable 18 months and, if nothing else I did depart with 600 odd hours of flying time in my log book and an extensive knowledge of the NW coast of Wales and the SW coast of Scotland including the Mull of Galloway and the Mull of Kintyre. I departed for pastures new on the 1st of January 1945 wondering what the next 18 months would bring.

RAF Wing

Wing in Bedfordshire was the next port of call. It was No.26 OTU (Operational Training Unit) and I found myself part of a crew of 6 flying in Wellington Aircraft, generally known as "Wimpeys". The training we did was mostly cross country navigational exercises. In fact, similar to what I had been doing for the previous 18 months, but, with the greater range of the Wellington, trips now averaged 5 or 6 hours duration. At 22 years of age, I was the oldest member of the crew and also the most experienced, with more actual flying time than the other 5 added together. My job was more or less the same as my work at Millom, but rather easier as I did not have a trainee to guide through the various procedures. We did all the fringe bits and pieces of course, Dinghy Drill, Simulation High Altitude chamber etc. I do not remember anything very special about this period, apart perhaps from a couple of trips over Normandy, (the war had by this time moved into Germany). My memories are of seeing all the dead livestock lying in the fields waiting for someone to come along and clear up. The only other point is that I had now reached the somewhat exalted rank of "Warrant Officer", a rank I was able to exploit to the full during the rest of the time I still had to remain in the RAF.

RAF Acaster Malbis

Mid-April 1945 saw me on the move again – going on leave to await instructions as to where to report next, normal procedures meant that this would be a HCU (Heavy Conversion Unit), but that was not to be. My leave was constantly extended via a weekly telegram and a fortnightly pay voucher to be cashed at the post office. This went on for 3 or 4 weeks and during this time the war in Europe ended, leaving me wondering "what next?", for the war in the Far East was still being pursued. However, my instructions finally arrived and I was on my way to Acaster Malbis, a place I had never heard of, but was relieved to find it was only about 5 miles outside York.

I duly arrived there in early May to find that it had been a Bomber Command airfield which had been mothballed, but was now being re-opened to accommodate all the redundant aircrew who were in limbo. All channels now full as replacements were no longer required. All was chaotic initially with no one seeming to have much idea about what was going on, but we were being fed and watered and indeed paid. On this point perhaps I should mention that now, as a Warrant Officer, I no longer had to attend pay parade, I simply called in to the accounts dept. and signed for my cash. Really quite civilised. Some sort of order was eventually established, with interviewing panels set up to send individuals off in various directions and career changes. Some crews, and indeed the ones from my OTU course included, were posted off to Transport Command where there was much work still to be done. Unfortunately, I was now part of a headless crew, as my pilot (being Canadian) had been sent off down to Fleetwood where all the Canadians were being assembled to await transport home – as Canada no longer had any commitments, not being involved in the war in the Far East.

Thus ended my flying days. It was to be years before I would fly again, and next time, rather than being paid to fly, I had to pay to fly! Very different now from the sort of flying I had been accustomed to, now it is just a bus ride without the scenery. It was now interview time to discover where I would be going next. Returning to flying duties was not an option, there were just too many trained aircrew in the system The choices were somewhat limited, and I finally opted for a radar mechanics course. Two reasons: I thought the knowledge might be useful after the war with the possible advent of TV and I knew the course was down at Yatesbury where I had spent some time before and I rather fancied another spell there with the new freedom that I could enjoy as a Warrant Officer. Now it was a matter of waiting for a vacancy on a course, this took several weeks, and I rather enjoyed what remained of my time at Acaster.

RAF Yatesbury (again)

Thus the beginning of July 1945 saw me settling in down in Wiltshire. Nice homecoming in a way, and comfortable in the knowledge that all that cross country running was no longer a threat. I was actually in a unique situation, as the remainder of my group were all new recruits, subject of course to all the parade ground stuff and other pastimes that passed for initial training. With my new rank I could avoid all this and I went on to exploit my new situation to the full. Classroom work and technical work in the labs was the general order of things. I made a point of attending those but nothing else. In the classrooms I found we were on a course of mathematics, and I rather enjoyed the opportunity to extend my somewhat elementary knowledge of that subject. I also picked up a few bits of know how in the workshops, e.g. using a soldering iron for much finer work than that met with a couple of years earlier at No.7 signals school. I also learned to use a Vernier, a Micrometer, and a slide rule – skills not much in demand these days. Apart from course work, my time was my own and this I spent between my quarters (I had my own room again), the mess, and later in the day the Lansdowne Hotel down in Calne. With a break for tea in one of the cafes, which all seemed to be owned by Harris's – (the well known pie merchants). All things considered it was an enjoyable period. In retrospect I suppose my life then was equivalent to that of a college student today – only turning up in the training wing when I thought it was worthwhile, with the advantage of course that I did not have any financial obligations. This all came to an end when the war in the Far East ended, and forces requirements were again reviewed, with information starting to come through about demobilisation dates.

The radar course that I was on was a long one of two years duration, split into ten week segments. I had just finished the first one and learned that I had the option of taking a shorter course, or signing on for five more years and completing the course. Five more years was too much to contemplate and so I settled for a driving course lasting six weeks. I thought that this might prove useful and interesting, and would give me a driving licence when I eventually got out. Also the driving school was at Weeton nr. Blackpool, handy for weekends at home.

RAF Lyneham

After two or three weeks I was on my way again, this time to Lyneham in Wiltshire, which then was, and still is, a large transport airfield, and I actually thought I was about to resume flying duties, but I was sadly mistaken.

Arrived at Lyneham to find that I was unexpected (again!) and by now I was beginning to think that no one wanted to know me any more, not that I was too concerned. I quickly found myself some comfortable quarters, booked in to the accounts dept (just to make sure the money kept coming in), and checked out the local geography, i.e. the way to the nearest pub. I then sat back and waited for the next development. Nice relaxing time really, but I was soon on the move again, February 1946 found me on my way at last to my driving course.

This proved to be quite enjoyable, with a gradual progression from 16hp cars up to 5 ton heavy goods vehicles. The driving part was only 2 hours per day. I made use of my rank again and did not participate in any of the other activities. I also took advantage of the fact that I was close to home and went there every Friday night for the weekend – all very sociable. Finally passed out, now with a licence to drive anything apart from articulated vehicles, and on my way on leave again to wait to see what my next move would be. I knew at this stage that it wouldn't be long before I was saying goodbye to the RAF, as it was possible to roughly estimate when my number for demobilisation would come up. I thought about mid-summer which turned out to be about right, my number was 41.

RAF Handforth

The telegram with instructions duly arrived, and I found that I was to report to the MT section at 61 MU Handforth. This sounded ideal and I cycled down to book in and make arrangements to live out. I thought this would be a good introduction to civilian life; living at home and cycling to work, but events were to take another, and final turn. I introduced myself to the MT officer in charge, a gentleman by the name of Quant who took an immediate dislike to me, which was reciprocated, I don't think he really wanted me in his department, difficult for him I suppose as I was still carrying my Warrant Officer rank but now only employed as a driver. Still there was nothing he could do about it, my rank was sacrosanct and I was still getting rank pay and flying pay.

I collected the lorry allocated to me. It was a somewhat worse for wear Canadian 3 ton Dodge. Difficult to drive and requiring constant double declutching and gear changing just to get up the smallest of inclines. That said, it had to do. On checking the work schedules I found that there was the odd load to be picked up and taken over to 7 site (which I discovered was in Adlington) where the Industrial Estate is now, which I thought would be ideal for me. So I used my rank again to establish myself as the regular driver covering 7 site. Handforth was overloaded with equipment for storage and made use of several sites over a wide area to store surplus materials – 99% of which was never used and would end its life in some scrap yard somewhere but it had to be stored and documented. I remember on one occasion taking a load of Lancaster spares to Woodford (Avro's as it was then). At first they refused to accept it, but eventually realised they had no alternative, and took it to some far off hangar. They too were getting desperate for space, for no longer required parts were still coming off the production lines.

I made the most of my daily runs to 7 site, usually going home first after collecting my vehicle from the yard and having an early morning break before going to the site to check if there was anything to move before going back to the main site for lunch. Another run to Adlington in the afternoon, before returning to the yard, parking up and going home. I often saw the MT officer watching me through his office window and looking quite concerned. Don't know why, as although I was usually the last one to leave the yard at the start of the day, I made up for this by being the first one back in the evening. One afternoon a week was given over to vehicle washing, but as there were a few Italian prisoners of war working in the yard. It was quite possible to get a good job done for the price of a packet of cigarettes, with half to get the job started and the other half on completion. It was just a case of sit in the mess until they came to tell me that the job was finished. This rather comfortable period came to a sudden end when I was summoned to see the MT officer to be informed of my next move. He informed me that I was to be posted to Wickenby, which was a storage site for the main depot; to go there and take charge of the MT section. (I think he was pleased to have the opportunity to get rid of me!) My old Dodge had finally given up the previous afternoon, pronounced irreparable and presumably written off, but I was pleased with the replacement, a two ton Austin Tender straight from the factory, similar to a pick-up and a delight to drive.

I picked the truck up the following morning, called at home to collect my gear, and set off to Wickenby – which I ascertained was a disused airfield about seven miles east of Lincoln. When I arrived it was to discover all signs of flying had long gone. Hangers were full to bursting point with spares that were no longer in demand. On further investigation I discovered that the MT section consisted of one other truck and one driver, a young lad only recently called up. Further enquiries produced some unexpected results. We were a mixed group of about 23 or 24, with 3 cooks, 3 telephonists, and a larger number of armourers making safe and disposing of bombs, ammunition, and other military hardware that was still lying around. I was informed that an administrative officer had been in overall charge until the previous day when he had left to be demobbed, but his replacement had failed to arrive. As a warrant officer with no other senior officers on the station, I had become de-facto the commanding officer of the whole establishment. A most unusual situation, but one which was to become quite interesting.

It soon became clear that I was also responsible for seeing that everyone got paid, relieving the telephonist when one of their number was absent on leave, and so providing short term cover. Although there was very little traffic, the telephone line had to be kept open 24 hours a day. I did make full use of this facility to make a few private calls. Rations were collected every other day from a depot in Market Rasen and, as we were such a small group these were more than adequate. We all dined together and really lived very well. I went over myself for the rations or occasionally sent my one and only driver. There was also a daily run to Wragby to pick up any post, as postal services were no longer available. Pay day became my responsibility and involved a trip over to Scampton to collect the money along with a list with the amounts due to everyone. This only happened a couple of times as I was only there a few weeks. On returning with the cash I was wondering how I could get in touch with all as they were scattered around the airfield. I needn't have worried as the bush telegraph had been at work and all and sundry were waiting around the MT office when I returned.

One unusual occurrence that I have a vivid memory of was concerning the main runway, now out of use of course. There were a team of contractors working at one end making repairs to the surface, whilst at the far end of the same runway were another group engaged in digging it up, taking all the surface material away and ploughing up the land prior to it being returned to agricultural use. This all seemed very odd to say the least, so I enquired as to why the repair work was still going on. The reply, and I quote *"The contract still has two years to run"*, unbelievable! I often wondered what the outcome would be when the two groups met, but I was long gone before then.

I made full use of my new found power as MT officer, e.g. I made a habit of driving home for most weekends on Friday evening I armed myself with suitable cover notes to cover my journeys, one for the trip home and another for the return journey on Sunday night. To say that I was picking stores up to take to store at Wickenby. I should perhaps mention that the cover note was a form to cover all transportation, with 3 sections, one requesting transport and saying why needed (this I duly signed as Commanding Officer), the second part to be signed by the MT officer and stamped with the official stamp, (this I complied with), and the third part to be signed by the driver on completion of the journey (this I duly signed on my return) then I filed the form, don't know why! Fuel was never a problem as I had sole access to the one remaining pump. When I was home for the weekend, I parked the lorry in a disused sandpit behind my home in case anyone passing became curious. On my return on Sunday evening, I stopped off in Lincoln, parked in the station yard, and went into the nearest pub to await the arrival of the last London train. There were always one or two people travelling up from points south who had been on weekend leave, looking for a lift back to Wickeriby. Generally speaking the whole establishment ran very smoothly, everyone getting on with their own jobs and waiting for the next pay day!

De-mobbed at last

My time at Wickenby passed very quickly and the time when I would part company with the RAF was fast approaching. My demob number (41) came up in early June 1946. The 11th found me on my on my way down to Uxbridge to go through the demobilisation process. I collected my civilian suit (not much choice, there were a lot of look-a-likes walking around). I could have a cap or trilby, mac or overcoat, grey or fawn suit all parcelled up in a cardboard box. All back pay was collected, plus civilian documents and ration book. Uniform handed in, apart from that being worn. I received a one-way ticket for the journey home. Now I was on my way on a month's demob leave, finally severing all links with the RAF in mid-July – just before my 24th birthday. A final twist when I was on the train on the way to Manchester. An airman got into my compartment, it was my soon to be Brother-in-law, also carrying his little box.

Life in 'Civvy Street' was now very close. I had to seriously rethink my lifestyle, with an immediate 50% reduction in pay, my own clothes and food to buy, and very soon a young family to be responsible for.

On reflection, I have to think that my uniform years had been a rewarding experience, having seen and done many things that would have been outside my orbit, yet of course, I had been very lucky. So many of my acquaintances and indeed friends had perished over the skies of Europe. Now it was farewell to the uniform times, and I could finally shape my own destiny about where and when. In short I was no longer just a number.

A. Dudley 2000

An Ode to Walney Airfield, 1940

The following poem was written at North Scale in 1940 at the time of the construction of Walney Airfield. Whilst this certainly wouldn't win any literary prizes, it does name some of the people who helped to build the airfield in those dark years. For this alone it is a valuable record. My late Father, who was the Timekeeper for John Laing & Son, is mentioned in the first verse.

DAWN

When dawn breaks out on Walney, Fred Edge he starts the day
He blows his whistle so loudly it is heard in Morecambe Bay.

Taylor's the first arrival, his number is a thousand and one,
But this is a rare occasion - a thing that is seldom done.

Soon the clang of the shovels can be heard all over the site
For the navvies have left their hovels to work with all their might.

Then up comes a little black Austin and out steps Mr Gass
Who says its very exhausting to follow behind an ass!

We all know who the ass is, it's that stout old checker Cook
For he utters "Nay be B'ggared" when confronted by a spook.

The spook is the one-eyed Watchman, yes the Fire-Bucket sort,
He tell you tales of chivalry and of the battle he thought that he'd fought.

Do you want the bucket? Is his working cry.
What's this all about the fire watchers shout
But it isn't for the Fire-bombs - it's to save you going out!

Then there's old Perce the Janitor, an attendant fit tor a King
He shuffles along like a matador, hoping that cracked cups will ring.

He is also a cricketer, a sportsman, have no doubt,
But you should hear the laughter when the first ball bowls him out.

There is also three young ladies to brighten the office here,
We often call them other names when they aren't here to hear!

Also there's Mr Adcock, Cashier upon this job
He's got to fill the packets for the hard working mob.

Then there is young Clifford, his smile you'll all agree
Seems to brighten the office with that morning cup of tea.

Then we have a Sandy, a Manager on the site
Not the BBC organist that we listen to at night. (Sandy Mae Pherson)

He's a Scot that swears a lot when levels don't agree
He'll try a peg in another spot and have to uproot a tree!

Then out goes the Surveyors lightly with rods and Dumpy all
To smite the Scot so mighty as David did for Saul.

Then we've Brother Riding, who plays the organ sweet
With strains of joyous tidings to keep us off the streets.
You have often heard of Shackley he's the fitter on this site
A mender up of Dumper trucks, a fireman by right.

A cap pulled down upon his crown and hairs upon his chest,
And oil and grease all up and down he is a B***** Mess!

Ah! but we have a costing office and its often said
If it wasn't for our prattle the office would seem dead.

But who is the lad with the curly mop, reminds one of a turnip top
He wanted to be a flying ace but found he couldn't keep the pace.
(Ian Howell)

Now that the poem is ended and to those who have taken part
We hope that you're not offended at this magnificent piece of art.

Finis

Donated by Brian Edge of Crewe, Cheshire

Mr F.W. Ramsay — 1942/43

At the beginning of 1942, Training Command were unable to get what were termed as "Screened Aircrew". This meant aircrew who had completed a tour of operations and were due to be rested. These crews were being kept at Operational Training Units etc. which came under Bomber Command, so Training Command decided to train their own Staff Crews.

RAF Millom & beyond

In June 1942 I was one of 21 Wireless Operators who were posted in to RAF Millom. Being a Fleetwood lad, this was a good posting for me as I was able to go home on my days off. Once we had passed our Air Operating Course at Millom we did a month's Gunnery Training at RAF Walney. I enjoyed this a great deal. We trained on the Boulton Paul Defiant Aircraft, and after passing out with "Wings and Stripes" at the end of July 1942, I returned to RAF Millom to join the station's staff.

I was married whilst serving at Millom, on the 19th December 1942. With my aircrew leave and days off I spent a happy Christmas at home, but was feeling a bit fed up as I caught the last train back to Millom.

I was even more fed up when I was told that I had been posted to RAF Wigtown with effect from the next morning! I was only at Wigtown two months when they opened a new station to train Staff Pilots at RAF Cark. I can honestly say that I enjoyed every minute of my stay at Cark. I was posted there as a Sgt and left as a Warrant Officer for an Operational Training Unit.

From OTU. I was eventually crewed up and we were posted to RAF Luffenham for training on the four engine heavy Lancaster Bombers. As we finished our course, VE Day was declared. Bomber Command found themselves redundant and that was the last of my flying.

I was posted to RAF Kirkham (now Kirkham Prison) for an equipment assistants course which I completed before being de-mobbed in March 1946.

Fred Ramsay 2000

Sgt Fred Ramsay (extreme right, front row)

RAF Cark 1943

Photo: F.Ramsay

The Story of Griff and May by Barbara Huxley

LACW May Ledson

This is the story of Flying Officer Oscar Griffiths and May Chatten. I am Barbara Huxley, daughter of May, and the story that I wish to tell has emerged over a period of several years. It is a story of World War II, 100 Squadron and the effects of war on two young people back in 1944 and, indeed others including myself, in recent years. The generosity of many people who have helped me to unearth the story of my mother and her wartime love for Oscar Griffiths has truly astounded me. I wish to thank all those who have given me, and May, their time and memories.

One evening in April 1943, LACW May Ledson was on duty in the control tower at Number 10 Air Gunnery School, RAF Walney Island. On the floor above was a young pilot Flt Sgt Oscar Griffiths (also known as Griff) who hailed from Swansea in South Wales. Griff came down the stairs and, spotting May at work, introduced himself. May had not previously met him, but had typed his name onto Pilot Duty Lists many times. They chatted to each other and Griff asked May if he could walk her back to WAAF quarters at the end of their duty shift. The spark was ignited, and what follows is, quite literally, history. During what remained of Griff's tour at Walney Island, they spent much of their free time together. Romance blossomed as Griff and May walked around the island coastline together singing as they crossed the Barrow bridge to the Imperial Hotel for crumpets with jam (no butter, there was a war on!) Griff, who had completed pilot training in Canada, was awaiting posting to Bomber Command and gained further experience by flying aircraft at Walney as part of the Air Gunners training programme. Griff's expected posting was soon ordered, and he and May were sad at their parting but like many young couples of that era, they made plans to marry at the end of the war. Griff was posted to RAF Hemswell Heavy Conversion Unit (HCU) to convert to the Lancaster, and then on to RAF

Flt Sgt Oscar Griffiths 10AGS

Waltham (Grimsby) and 100 Squadron in 1944. Whilst at HCU Griff was commissioned as a Pilot Officer and he telephoned May asking her how she would like to go out with an officer. May was thrilled and Griff made the long journey back to Walney to see her again. Then it was operational duty with 'The Ton'. May had sewn his 'wings' onto his tunic and had included the words "Happy Landings" on the reverse side of the brevet - the aircrew toast! Griff and May wrote regularly to each other and met whenever they managed to obtain a 48 hour pass. May loved receiving his letters – poetic and beautifully written. In one he told May that he "would always return to her and bloom again like a rose after the winter". Waltham was a happy base and Griff loved the crew that he had formed when joining 'The Ton'. In October 1944, May travelled to Waltham but Griff was detailed to fly an operation at short notice. So it was in the early hours of the morning when he returned that they were able to walk the lanes around Waltham and Holton-le-Clay in the wind and the rain. Griff's crew, also out walking after their return, spotted them and made the comment that it was a "...terrible night Skip" to which Griff's reply was "...it's a lovely way to spend an evening!" Griff and his crew went on to fly 29 'ops' and were due to be rested at 'tour-ex' after the next mission.

On Christmas Eve 1944, Griff and his crew took off for Cologne, on what should have been their final 'op' in their usual aircraft ND388 HW-G. The bombing run was good. The target of Nippes railway yard was hit, and Griff turned for home. Tragedy then struck and the aircraft, after being hit by flak, was destroyed with all crew members lost. They are all at rest in the beautifully kept War Cemetery at Rheinberg in Germany. May had lost her Griff, and it would seem that this should be the end of our story but there is more to come.

May was de-mobbed in 1946, and the pain of losing Griff eased with time. May married Harry and had two children, myself and brother Ian. Subsequently five grandchildren were followed by a great grandchild with another on the way. May was happy, but she didn't forget Griff. When May was in her seventies, she visited Walney Island again taking me along. She found that the control tower, where she had met Griff all those years ago, was still standing. She went in and the memories came flooding back. May walked around the Nissen huts and what remained of the other wartime buildings, half expecting Griff to appear out of the mists of time. It was in 2011, some 67 years after May had first met Griff, that she received a letter from Michael Gill. Michael's mother, who died when he was just five years old, was also a WAAF based at Walney and he was searching for people who might have known her. May had known her, and subsequently met Michael to tell him what she knew of his mother. Michael was a mine of information about Walney and this kindled a desire in May to find out more about the loss of HW-G and whether Griff had any relations still living. May told me much more about her time with Griff, and this spurred me to become involved with May's search. I began the search via Jim Stewart of BBMF and also made contact with two members (Brian Hulme and Dr Keith Ellis) of 100 Squadron Association. The help and assistance from the Association has been unstinting and so generous. I then made contact with The Swansea Evening News and their reporter, Geraint Thomas, ran a full page spread on the story of May and Griff. The very next day I received a phone call from a school friend of Griffs, Gordon Dennis, and he in turn helped me to make contact with Wynne – a nephew of Griffs. A letter then arrived from Howell Evans, a mid-upper gunner from 100 Squadron (and later 550 Squadron at North Killingholme), who had also flown on the Cologne raid that fateful Christmas Eve of 1944. He provided crystal clear details of the events of that night. Both Gordon and Howell, now in their late 80's, regularly write to and phone May. Surprisingly, the three people who made the initial contact with us were Howell, Wynne and Gordon - HW-G! Other people who have got in touch include the sister of Griff's mid-upper gunner [James Islwyn Morgan] and the secretary of the chapel in Gowerton attended by the Griffiths family (who also sent us a photograph of a memorial plaque to Griff in the chapel). It would really complete the circle of fate if May were able to find someone who actually knew, and can remember, Griff during his time with 100 Squadron at Waltham*.

F/O Oscar Griffiths (centre)
with 5 of his Lancaster crew at OTU

RAF Coningsby 1944. On left F/O Griffiths (pilot) and crew (order unknown) Sgt Dawson (engineer), Sgt Cozens (navigator), W/O Krewenchuk (bomb aimer), Flt Sgt McGuire (w/op), Sgt Morgan (mid upper gunner), Sgt Frank Crompton (rear gunner)

*Information can be passed via the author's website www.johnnixonauthor.co.uk

May Ledson shown here with Battle of Britain memorial flight Lancaster during a poignant visit to RAF Coningsby in 2012.

Photo Mike Gill.

WAAF E.G. OWEN 2102560
by her son, Mike Gill

In October 1942, my mother Edith Owen (nee Gill) enlisted into the WAAF. She was posted to 10 AGS at Walney Isle in November that year. Her role at 10 AGS was that of 'Flight Mechanic Airframes', repairing Ansons.

1 don't know much about my mother's service life, as sadly she passed away when I was 5 years old, but do I remember my father telling me she lied about her age in order to enlist. This was confirmed when I applied to the RAF records office in Gloucester for a copy of her service record. This confirmed what my father had told me, as it stated her DOB as 1924, whereas she was born in 1927!

Over the years, I have managed to contact a few WAAFs that served at Walney who knew my mother. One such WAAF was a good friend called May Ledson. May worked in the control tower so didn't see my mother on a work basis, but she saw her often when they rehearsed for one of the many shows that were put on at Barrow. May sang and performed on stage and my mother was involved in the costumes and scenery. One such show was called 'Bang On' and was performed at His Majesty's Theatre at Barrow, commencing in May 1945. May told me they had a great time at these shows and they had many a laugh backstage with the cast and crew. This show must have meant a lot to my mother as she kept a lot of photos, cuttings and tickets (signed by her friends) relating to it. My mother, stayed at 10 AGS until December 1944 when she was then posted to 11 AGS and was de-mobbed in September 1946.

Mike Gill and Peter Yuile, Sunderland air show 2011

E.G. Owen's Scrap Book Memories of her time at RAF Walney
(preserved by her son Mike Gill)

Outside stage door at
His Majesty's Theatre Barrow-in-Furness
(Edith Owen on right, May Ledson centre)

Spitfire and Wellington

Edith Owen standing 4th from right in front of 10AGS Wellington

Unknown group standing in front of 1OAGS Wellington

LAC Bryce (left) with unknown pal.
Photo sent to Edith with caption on back...
'To Darky, best wishes, love from a pal at Walney Josie Bryce.'

Edith Owen 2nd from right

RAF Walney's theatrical troupe

R.A.F. Score Direct Hit For Charities

There was only one complaint to be made anent the opening performance of "Bang On," the Walney R.A.F. newest production, on the stage at His Majesty's Theatre, Barrow, this week.

The complaint was that very familiar ex-war complaint: There was not enough of it. Though it was a ful two-hours show, with every minute packed with entertainment—as streamlined and almost as swift as the Raf's own Spitfires. And one wanted more.

It would be more than invidious, it would be difficult to measure the comparative merits of the tuneful music, and graceful dancing, the sparkling humour and originality, or to separate the superb dressing and the brilliant settings or the colourful spectacle.

One item of which one could have stood much more was "The Opera Shop"—a potted "drama" of a store's rise and fall, told in cleverly written parodies set to the music of famous opera airs—and brilliantly sung by almost the entire company.

Superb burlesque of real wit was provided by John Kirlew, either as "Winifred Clifford the WAAF" or "Nina Conchita the spy." The same player combined with Bill Finlay and John Wilkinson in a Grecian "episode" of laughter merit—with bar!

SUPERB VOCALISM.

But few shows have been graced by such all-round excellence in the singing. There was always delight, whether in the ringing baritone of Cledwyn Jones or the lighter, but finely dramatic baritone of Jack Sewart, in the silver bell clarity of Patricia Garvey's mezzo-soprano or the superb flexibility of Kathleen Harris's soprano who moved easily from "crooning" to a fine dramatic aria from "Madame Butterfly."

Joe Clements, the c/o and D/o with their banjos; Bill Finlay and Don Hudson, with a piano; May Ledson and Ruth Fleming; Joe Watkins, Catherine Whittaker—all were speciality acts with equal claims to the " top of the bill."

Aided more than a little by the tuneful arrangements of Don Hudson, the R.A.F. station orchestra also performed brilliantly, and were matched by the modern swing style of the "Modernaires" and "Doreen."

The whole was set in the brilliant decor of Steve Sherlock, with assistants Bill Epworth and George Skinner and of the dressing it is sufficient to say that among the gowns were a number loaned by the Gainsborough Film Studios. Dance ensembles were arranged to fine effect by Catherine Whittaker.

His Majesty's (or Her Majesty's – both used depending on who was on the throne) was previously The Theatre Royal, which was sited on Albert Street, Barrow-in-Furness. The name changed in 1905 and kept going as HM for 50 years.
Information courtesy of Lorraine Wrennall.

Christmas greetings to Edith from afar.

SEASON'S GREETINGS

1612954 SGT. WINTER.
S.H.Q.
R.A.F. PADANG.
SUMATRA.

To Darky & Doreen,
wishing you both a very happy Xmas – wish I could be there.

Jack.

P.S. How's about the odd few lines??

THIS IS FOR BOTH OF YOU!!

XMAS AIR LETTER RAFPOST
POSTAGE FREE
SOUTH EAST ASIA

Xmas Air Letters may be despatched POSTAGE FREE to U.K., EIRE, B.L.A., U.S.A. and all BRITISH EMPIRE COUNTRIES and FORCES and will be forwarded by air throughout for delivery as possible.

Xmas Air Letters are subject to Unit Censorship (where in force)

UNIT CENSOR STAMP

20 NOV 45
SOUTH EAST ASIA

R.A.F. Postal Services and Welfare.

It is difficult to imagine a white Christmas in Sumatra!

10AGS group of friends on Walney beach

Edith as bridsmaid at friend's wedding

All Services march through Barrow-in-Furness 1944
(parade started in Hindpool Rd & marched down Michaelson Rd)

Photos Edith Owen (Mike Gill's collection)

SECTION SIX

Relics and Reminders

Walney Airfield remains today as one of the finest surviving examples of a World War II 'expansion' period installations in the North West of England. This is due to the continued usage of its surviving runways and infrastructure from the time of its closure to the present day. The following photographs serve to illustrate what airfield architecture has survived from its closure in 1947 up to the present day.

The photo above, taken on the 25th of July 1947, shows the control tower and flight buildings of, a then slumbering, RAF Walney. The photo below, taken a decade later, on the 2nd of July 1957, shows a deserted airfield already beginning to lose some of its buildings

Flight waiting room, control tower and fire tender shelter
2nd July 1957

Over the years Walney has played host to several airshows.
An Argus MII (G-AIYO) Seen here making a low-pass over the assembled crowds
28th August 1955

Photos P.G. Yuile's collection

Contemporary photographs courtesy of Mr Peter Yuile and Duggie Fisher.

Machine gun range stop-butts

WAAF site picket post

WAAF site ablution block

WAAF site picket post

WAAF site wooden hut
(last building to be demolished & is now the site of a nature garden)

Substation transformer building

Dedicated to the memory of these airmen, who were killed in flying accidents whilst operating from Walney Island. Plus at least 10 others whose names are not recorded.

Sgt J. Krol	RAF	Pilot
Sgt C. Lambert	RAF	Trainee FE / AG
Sgt T.F. Elliott	RAAF	Pilot
LAC S. Cooper	RAF	Trainee FE / AG
P.O. T.F. Mackie	RAF	Pilot
Flt Sgt T.L. Goulter	RAAF	Pilot
Sgt. J. Blunden	RAF	Pilot
LAC D.Wilson	RAF	Trainee WOP / AG
Sgt Szot	RAF	Pilot
LAC O.R. Jolly	RAF	T.T.O.
Sgt J.B.G. Methren	RAF	Pilot
LAC Hosh	RAF	Trainee WOP / AG
Sgt Anderton	RAF	Pilot
F.O. Creed	RAF	AG Instructor
LAC Wilson	RAF	Trainee WOP / AG
LAC Hudson	RAF	Trainee WOP / AG
LAC Lenaghan	RAF	Trainee WOP / AG
LAC G.A. Bradshaw	RAF	Trainee FE / AG
Flt Sgt E.H. Ciurkot	RAF	Pilot
LAC Collins	RAF	T.T.O.
Sgt T.H. Allen	RAF	Pilot
P.O. H.L. Dumbleton	RAF	Pilot
Flt Sgt Jordan	RAF	Pilot
Sgt Cooke	RAF	
Sgt Conisbee	RAF	
W.O. Pyka	RAF	Pilot
Flt Sgt A.J. Wood	RAF	Pilot
W.O. J.W. Wilson	RAF	AG Instructor
Sgt J.L. Turner	RAF	Trainee WOP / AG
Sgt K. Jenkins	RAF	Trainee WOP / AG
W.O. L.Trzebiatowski	RAF	Pilot
W.O. Harris	RAF	AG Instructor
Sgt Drake	RAF	Trainee WOP / AG
Sgt Brennan	RAF	Trainee WOP / AG
Sgt Mc Millan	RAF	Trainee WOP / AG
F.O. Bob Gray	RAF	Pilot
Flt Lt Flower	RNZAF	AG Instructor

SECTION SEVEN

Walney Aircraft

Specifications & Technical data

There follows what is designed to give the less knowledgeable reader a pictorial and technical description of the aircraft types operated from RAF Walney during its service life.

The data includes wingspan, dimensions, power plant, performance and armament for:

BOULTON PAUL DEFIANT

WESTLAND LYSANDER

MILES MARTINET

MILES MASTER

AVRO ANSON

VICKERS WELLINGTON

SUPERMARINE SPITFIRE

The Boulton Paul Defiant

TECHNICAL DATA	Defiant MKII
MANUFACTURER	Boulton Paul Aircraft Ltd, Wolverhampton
USAGE	Two seat turret fighter
CONSTRUCTION	Metal fuselage / airframe
POWER PLANT	1 x Rolls Royce Merlin XX 1260HP
DIMENSIONS	Span 34′4″ | Length 35′4″ | Height 12′2″ | Wing 250$^{2'}$
WEIGHT (laden)	8,600 lb
PERFORMANCE	315mph at 16,000ft
ARMAMENT	4 x 0.303 Brownings in power operated turret

The prototype, Defiant K8310, made its initial flight on the 11th of August, 1937. The type was unique in that it was a fighter aircraft which carried a four gun turret capable of delivering considerable fire power to the rear, but with no forward firing armament at all. In early engagements, German pilots routinely mistook the aircraft for a Spitfire or a Hurricane. They would begin a textbook attack from above and behind, only to fly into a deadly barrage from the Defiant's four Browning machine guns. It was No.264 Squadron of RAF Manston, Kent, who first began to operate the Defiant. By the 31st of May, 1941 they had shot down no less than 65 German aircraft, many of these whilst protecting the evacuation of Dunkirk.

Due to its lack of forward firing weaponry the enemy very quickly began to beat the Defiant. Consequently, the type was withdrawn from daylight frontline service to be used successfully in a night fighter capacity and as gunships at Air Gunnery Schools such as Walney. It is interesting to note that by May, 1942, 150 Defiants had been fully converted into target towing aircraft with turret removed and winch gear added in its place. Only one example of the type remains in preservation to this day, housed in pristine condition in the RAF Museum at Hendon.

Last surviving Defiant N1671 - seen here in preservation at RAF Museum Hendon.
Photos courtesy RAF Hendon Librarian Gordon Leith

Boulton Paul Defiants Stationed at 10AGS RAF Walney

This is a complete list of all Defiants based at RAF Walney during the airfield's service life. Most of these aircraft had been posted in from other units around the country, and many had seen action in the early stages of the war. Listed are those where the Squadrons are known and details of enemy engagement certain.

L6957*	264 Squadron *(28/8/40 damaged HEINKEL III)*
L6986	264 Squadron
L7002	Data unknown
L7017	264 Squadron *(Fought in the Battle of Britain)*
N1539	Data unknown
N1540	151 Squadron
N1542	Data unknown
N1549	141 Squadron *(Fought in the Battle of Britain)*
N1551	Data unknown
N1552**	141 Squadron *(2 Heinkel IIIs destroyed 16/9/40)*
N1559	141 Squadron *(Fought in the Battle of Britain)*
N1577	264 Squadron
N1582	Data unknown
N1612	307 Squadron
N1630	264 Squadron *(Fought in the Battle of Britain)*
N1636	151 Squadron
N1637	Data unknown
N1647	256 & 125 Squadron
N1677	151 Squadron
N1682	307 Squadron
N1683	307 Squadron *(Fought in the Battle of Britain)*
N1691	256 Squadron
N1698	256 Squadron
N1700	410 Squadron
N1701	151 & 125 Squadron
N1732	173 Squadron
N1733	54 Squadron
N1735	127 & 286 Squadron
N1736	619 Squadron
N1737	611 Squadron
N1741	256 Squadron
N1742	Data unknown
N1744	256 Squadron
N1752	141 Squadron
N1758	Data unknown
N1764	307 Squadron, 2OAFU
N1808	151, 96, 410 Squadron
N1811	Data unknown
N1812	307, 256 Squadron
N3313	61, 264, 456 Squadron
N3317	64, 151 Squadron
N3321	255, 409 Squadron
N3326	264 Squadron
N3328	151 Squadron
N3335	255 Squadron
N3387	151 Squadron
N3396	65, 409 Squadron
N3421	151, 256, 277 Squadron & 60 OUT
N3428	125 Squadron
N3441	Data unknown
N3448	96 Squadron
N3449	Data unknown
N3459	151 & 125 Squadron
N3482	151 Squadron, 60 OUT
N3491	12 Squadron
N3502	Data unknown
N3504	Data unknown
N3505	11 Squadron
N3506	Data unknown
N3507	Data unknown
N3511	255, 409 Squadron

* RAF Rochford - Sgt/Pilot A.J. Lauder, Sgt V.R. Chapman

** P/O Waddingham, Sgt Cumbers

Defiant N1671 - Photo Gordon Leith

N3517	48, 410 Squadron
N3518	Data unknown
N3519	Data unknown
T3919	Data unknown
T3928	66, 141 Squadron
T3930	Data unknown
T3936	57, 409, 96 Squadron
T3940	614, 456, 125 Squadron
T3943	141, 256 Squadron
T3954	96 Squadron
T3981	256 Squadron
T3984	2 OAFU
T3987	Data unknown
T3988	17 Squadron
T3989	Data unknown
T4004	256, 153 Squadron
T4005	255, 125 Squadron
T4006	256 Squadron
T40334	Data unknown
T4039	Data unknown
T4043	20 Squadron
T4046	Data unknown
T4047	Data unknown
T4048	Data unknown
T4060	Data unknown
T4061	Data unknown

T4065	Data unknown
T4072	Data unknown
T4074	Data unknown
T4076	Data unknown
T4109	Data unknown
T4111	56 Squadron
T4119	Data unknown
AA283	610 Squadron
AA289	Data unknown
AA299	Data unknown
AA310	49 Squadron
AA321	64 Squadron
AA326	Data unknown
AA328	Data unknown
V1109	Data unknown
V1111	Data unknown
V1112	Data unknown
V1114	Data unknown
V1122	Data unknown
V1139	Data unknown
V1170	Data unknown
V1171	31 Squadron
V1173	Data unknown
V1179	69 Squadron

The Westland Lysander

TECHNICAL DATA	**Westland Lysander**
MANUFACTURER	Westland Aircraft Ltd, Yeovil, Somerset
USAGE	Two seat army cooperation
CONSTRUCTION	Metal structure, fabric covered
POWER PLANT	1 x 890hp Bristol Mercury XII radial engine
DIMENSIONS	Span 50′ | Length 30′6″ | Height 11′6″ | Wing 260$^{2\prime}$
WEIGHT (laden)	5,920 lb
PERFORMANCE	229mph at 10,000ft
ARMAMENT	2 x fixed 0.303 guns forward 2 x 0.303 guns manually operated in rear cockpit 6 x light bombs below stub wings

Known broadly and affectionately as the 'Lizzie', the Lysander became in 1938 the first monoplane to enter Army Co-Operation Units, where it replaced the Hawker Hector biplane. The prototype, K6127, first flew in June, 1936 and an order for 144 Lysanders was placed with Westland in September of that year.

The type first entered service with No.16 Squadron at RAF Old Sarum late in 1938. In the September, 1,939 Lysanders went to France with Nos 2, 4,13 and 26 Squadrons to carry out artillery spotting and reconnaissance duties. During the Dunkirk evacuations, Lysanders acquitted themselves well, dropping supplies to troops and carrying out attacks on enemy positions. It is a fact that the Lysanders of No.4 Squadron were among the last aircraft to remain in action before withdrawing back to England.

As the war progressed the aircraft continued to give excellent service in an Air-Sea rescue role and as a target tug. Of course the role for which it is best known is that of 'Moonlight Lizzie', dropping Special Operations Executive (SOE) agents behind enemy lines. Production of the Lysander ceased in January, 1942 after 1,368 had been built.

Westland Lysanders Stationed at 10AGS

Sadly we do not have a service history for these aircraft prior to their being posted to RAF Walney. Here is a list of serial numbers for the 30 aircraft of the type that served at 10AGS.

LYSANDERS
stationed at 10AGS

N1320	T1738
R9124	T1750
T1433	T1752
T1438	T1756
T1441	T1758
T1446	T1762
T1516	P9115
T1521	V9414
T1534	V9666
T1570	V9680
T1571	V9861
T1654	V9863
T1672	V9864
T1673	W6940
T1674	

Westland Lysander - Photos Ken Ellis collection

The Miles Martinet

TECHNICAL DATA	**Miles Martinet**
MANUFACTURER	Miles Aircraft Ltd, Woodley, Reading
USAGE	Two seat target tug
CONSTRUCTION	Wooden structure, plywood covered
POWER PLANT	1 x 870hp Bristol Mercury radial engine
DIMENSIONS	Span 39′ | Length 30′11″ | Height 11′7″ | Wing 238²′
WEIGHT (laden)	6,600 lb
PERFORMANCE	225mph at 4,500ft

MARTINETS
stationed at 10AGS

HP135	HP305
HP270	HP306
HP271	HP307
HP272	HP308
HP273	HP309
HP274	HP310
HP275	HP311
HP276	HP312
HP277	HP313
HP278	HP314
HP279	HP315
HP286	JN493
HP287	JN601
HP288	JN638
HP303	MS500

The Martinet was the first aircraft to enter service with the RAF and had been designed from the outset as a target tug.

The prototype, LR241, made its maiden flight on the 24th of April, 1942. The aircraft was designed to carry either a motorised or wind driven winch, which could carry and operate six flay and sleeve drogue targets. From 1942 until 1945 the type was in large scale production for the RAF, with 1,724 aircraft being built.

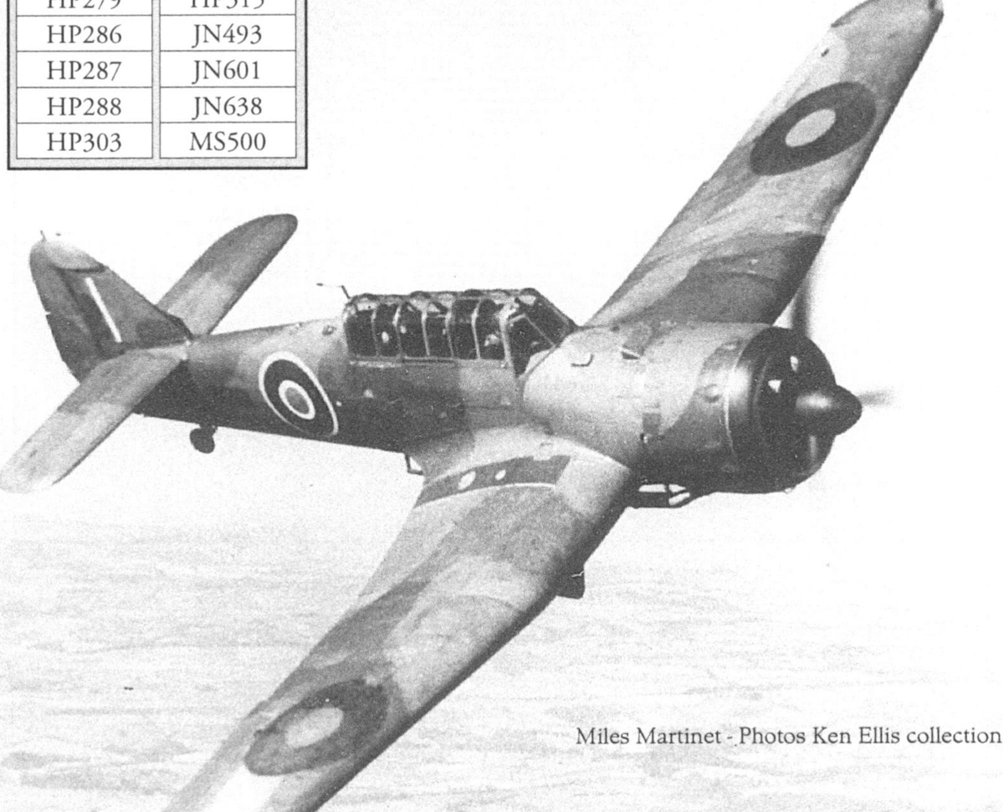

Miles Martinet - Photos Ken Ellis collection

The Miles Master

TECHNICAL DATA	**Miles Martinet**
MANUFACTURER	Miles Aircraft Ltd, Woodley, Reading
USAGE	2 seat advanced trainer
CONSTRUCTION	Wooden structure, plywood covered
POWER PLANT	1 x Pratt & Whitney Wasp Junior
DIMENSIONS	Span 35'7" | Length 30'2" | Wing 209$^{2'}$
WEIGHT (laden)	5,570 lb
PERFORMANCE	232mph at 7,200ft, range 320mls, service ceiling 27,300f
ARMAMENT	1 x fixed Vickers guns (forward firing Practice Bombs

The Master was developed from the earlier Miles Kestrel trainer.

The first prototype flew on the 10th November 1938 and the first of a final production run of 900 aircraft was taken on charge by the RAF in May 1939.

Miles Master - Photos Ken Ellis collection

The Avro Anson

TECHNICAL DATA	AVRO ANSON (Mk I)
MANUFACTURER	A.V.Roe & Co Ltd, Newton Heath, Chadderton & Yeadon.
USAGE	General Reconnaissance aircraft for crew of three
CONSTRUCTION	Metal fuselage, fabric covered, wooden wings and tail
POWER PLANT	2 x 350hp Armstrong Siddeley Cheetah 1 x radial engines
DIMENSIONS	Span 56'6" | Length 42'3" | Height 13'1" | Wing 410$^{2'}$
WEIGHT (laden)	8,000 lb
PERFORMANCE	188mph at 7,000ft
ARMAMENT	1 x fixed 0.303 guns forward 1 x 0.303 gun in turret Bomb load 360lbs

The first production Anson MKI (K6152) made its maiden flight on 31/12/35. A refinement and an advance on a design which had seen its inception a year previously, following the Air Ministry's request for a fighter bomber monoplane for operational use by the RAF.

On 6/3/36 a number of Ansons entered service with N°.48 Squadron at RAF Manston, Kent. This was to make the Avro Anson the first monoplane to enter squadrons under the RAF expansion scheme, and also the first aircraft to employ a retractable undercarriage – quite a novelty in 1936!

At the outbreak of war, the Anson remained on active service with Coastal Command. On 5/9/35 an Anson flying from N°.500 Squadron, RAF Detting, was responsible for the first RAF attack of the war on an enemy U-boat.

By 1940 the Anson was falling back from front line duties to be replaced by the Whitley and the Hudson, but on one creditable occasion in the summer of 1940, the Anson left no one in any doubt that it had teeth! In mid-June, over the English Channel, three Ansons not only survived an attack by nine ME109s, but succeeded in shooting down two of them and damaging another.

ANSONS
stationed at 10AGS

K6291	LT775
K8826	LT776
N5062	LT777
N5077	LT778
N5163	LT785
N9739	LT786
DG810	LT787
LT426	LT788
LT532	LT789
LT536	LT790
LT644	LT791
LT659	LT838
LT716	LV138
LT731	LV144
LT738	LV226
LT739	LV318
LT740	MG104
LT741	MG186
LT742	MG327
LT743	MG495
LT765	MG745
LT766	NK509
LT767	NK514
LT774	

Photo: Ken Ellis collection

It is from this point on that the Anson became widespread throughout Training Command. Giving good reliable service as an aircraft used to train wireless operators, air gunners, navigators and staff pilots; it earned itself the name 'faithful Annie' and is fondly remembered by veterans to this day.

K6183 - THE WORLD'S ONLY AIRWORTHY MK I ANSON

Alongwiththeworld'slastsurvivingDefiantatHendon'smuseumisthefuselage of MK I Anson WT068. Displayed upon the bed of an RAF transport trailer. Should one seek a complete example of the type Anson MKI N4877, it can be examined in pristine static condition in the airspace hall, Imperial War Museum, Duxford, Cambs. Now, due to the genius and hard work of Mr Bill Reid, his wife Robyn and their dedicated team at RR Aviation based in Nelson, New Zealand, the world has a flying example of the MK I Anson – once ubiquitous on airfields both in Britain and overseas.

Whist now bearing the serial number K6183, the aircraft was first given the number MH120 on 20/03/44 following its construction by Avro at Yeadon. Following which it was first issued to No.2 aircraft park, Bankstown NS Wales, where it was prepared for service with the RAAF. On 20/04/44 it was taken on charge by No.1 AOS Evans Head NSW. On 12/02/45 TX to Advanced Flying & Refresher Unit, Deniliquin. 03/10/45. Retired to Care & Maintenance unit, Deniliquin. 12/12/47 TX to No.1 Aircraft Depot, Laverton, Victoria for storage. 25/10/49 TX to No.2 Aircraft Depot, Richmond NSW. 23/02/50 Sold, struck off RAAF charge. Post RAAF re-registered as VHBLP and later VHBAF whilst used in civilian roles. In 1960 the aircraft was grounded following an undercarriage collapse but was back in the air by 1963.

Last restored to flying condition in the 1980s it was acquired by Bill Reid in 2002 and moved to New Zealand, where, following a superb restoration, it made its first flight on 17/07/12.

The photographs that follow offer the unique opportunity to provide an extensive illustration of the type both on the ground and in the air. I am deeply indebted to Mr Tony Clarry through whose kind offices I was able to acquire these photographs and to Mr Gavin Conroy who has very generously allowed me to use his excellent photographic work as part of this publication.

K6183
VX B
K6183

B VX
K6183

B
VX
K6183

VX
B
K6183

B
VX
K6183

The Vickers Wellington

TECHNICAL DATA	VICKERS WELLINGTON
MANUFACTURER	Vickers Armstrong Ltd, Weybridge, Chester & Blackpool
USAGE	Long range night bomber for crew of 6
CONSTRUCTION	Metal geodite structure, fabric covered
POWER PLANT	2 x Bristol Pegasus engines
DIMENSIONS	Span 86′ | Length 64′7″ | Height 17′5″ | Wing $840^{2'}$
WEIGHT (laden)	29,000 lb
PERFORMANCE	255mph at 15,000ft, service ceiling 19,000ft
ARMAMENT	2 x 0.303 guns in nose turret 4 x 0.303 guns in rear turret 2 x 0.303 guns manually operated Bomb load 4,500lbs

For a long period following the outbreak of World War II, the Wellington could quite accurately be described as the mainstay of Bomber Command. Of the 1,000 bomber raids on Cologne in May, 1942 half the aircraft taking part were Wellingtons. Known by the RAF and public alike as the 'Wimpey' or 'Ton', the aircraft was of a very robust design indeed. Featuring a lattice-work geodetic construction, it was able to absorb and survive heavy punishment at the hands of the German flak batteries.

WELLINGTONS
stationed at 10AGS

X3600	LP946
X3885	LP962
BJ900	LP964
BK208	LP974
HE742	LP981
HF487	JN461
HF744	JN502
HZ272	ME982
LN450	NA741
LP662	NA827
LP764	NC780
LP879	NC801
LP883	NC803
LP887	NC825
LP924	NC827
LP925	NC867
LP945	NC951

Prototype Wellington K4049 first flew on the 15th of June, 1936 powered by two Bristol Pegasus engines. The Air Ministry were sufficiently impressed as to place an initial order for 180 aircraft.

The Wellington was one of the first allied aircraft to bomb German targets. On the 1st of April, 1944 it also became the first to drop the newly developed 4,000lb 'black buster' bomb during a raid on Emden.

A versatile design, the Wellington was to serve at home and overseas with distinction. It was employed on Coastal Command duties, reconnaissance, in Transport Command and in Training Command long after it was superseded by the four engine 'heavies' for front line duty.

Vickers Wellington - Photo Ken Ellis collection

Vickers Wellington - Photo Author's collection

The Supermarine Spitfire

TECHNICAL DATA	**Spitfire MKI + MKII**
MANUFACTURER	Vickers Armstrong Ltd, Supermarine division
USAGE	Single seater fighter
CONSTRUCTION	All-metal 'monocoque' body
POWER PLANT	880hp Rolls Royce Merlin
DIMENSIONS	Span 36'10" | Length 29'11" | Height x'x" | Wing $242^{2'}$
WEIGHT (laden)	5,784 lb
PERFORMANCE	357mph at 19,000ft
ARMAMENT	4 x 0.303 machine guns 2 x 20mm cannons

SPITFIRES
stationed at 10AGS

P7283	W3253
P7440	W3608
P7521	W3823
P7673	W3828
P7851	AB812
P8081	AD451
P8131	AD464
P8174	AR323
P8248	BL591
P8260	BM298
P8513	BM423
P8659	BM630
W3209	EP651

An aviation legend, an icon and almost every schoolboys first Airfix kit, this aircraft needs little introduction. Prototype K5054 made its maiden flight on the 5th of March, 1936 and the design handled like a thoroughbred from the very start – cresting amazement whenever it was demonstrated.

Production of the Spitfire MK1 began at the Supermarine factory in 1937. Initially it was armed with 0.303 machine guns. Although, by the time that the type saw action in the Battle of Britain, thought was being devoted to fitting the fighter with heavy cannons.

In February, 1939 a Spitfire was fitted experimentally with two 20mm cannons. The aircraft successfully destroyed a DO17 (Dornier 17 aircraft) in March, 1940. The experiment was a success and the beginning of a legend.

Miscellaneous Aircraft Stationed at 10AGS

AIRCRAFT	Serial	Description
AVRO MANCHESTER	L7283	held as instructional airframe
BLACKBURN BOTHA	L6229	
HAWKER HENLEY	L3264	
HAWKER HENLEY	L3333	
MILES MAGISTER	T9768	
DE HAVILLAND DOMINIE	X7368	
DE HAVILLAND GYPSY MOTH	DG579	previously GAAFI requisitioned by RAF at outset of war

Avro Manchester (Ken Ellis collection)

Hawker Henley

Gypsy Moth

Blackburn Botha

Miles Magester (with Cark CO)

DH Dominie (Ken Ellis collection)

Index

M

N

O

P

R

S

T

U

V

W

Y

GLOSSARY

AACU......Anti aircraft Co-operation Unit
AGS.........Air Gunnery School
AOS.........Air Observer School
ATA.........Air Transport Auxiliary
ATC.........Air Training Corps
AC1.........Aircraftman 1st Class
AC2.........Aircraftman 2nd Class
AOAFU...Air Observer Advanced Flying Unit

BGS.........Bombing and Gunnery School
CO..........Commanding Officer
Cpl..........Corporal
Cpt..........Captain
DFI..........Direction Finding Indicator
DFC........Distinguished Flying Cross
DSO........Distinguished Service Order
EFTS........Elementry Flying Training School
EATP.......Empire Air Training Programme
EOTS.......Equipment Officers Training School

F/O..........Flying Officer
Flt/Lt.......Flight Lieutenant
Flt/Sgt......Flight Sergeant
FAA..........Fleet Air Arm
Flt/Eng.....Flight Engineer
FTS..........Flying Training School
GRP.........Group
HCU........Heavy Conversion Unit
HMS........His Majesty's Ship
ITS...........Initial Training School
LAC.........Leading Aircraftman
LAU.........Light Artilliery Unit

MOD.......Ministry of Defence
MU..........Maintenance Unit
NCO.......Non Commissioned Officer
OCU........Operational Conversion Unit
OTU........Operational Training Unit
ORB........Operational Record Book
OAF.........Observer Advanced Flying Unit
P/O..........Pilot Officer
POW........Prisoner of War
PR...........Photographic Reconnaissance
RAF.........Royal Air Force
RPAF.......Royal Polish Air Force
RAAF.......Royal Australian Air Force
RCAF.......Royal Canadian Air Force
RN..........Royal Navy
RNAS......Royal Naval Air Station
RFC.........Royal Flying Corps
RVVR......Royal Naval Volunteer Reserve
S/Sgt........Staff Sergeant
Sgt...........Sergeant
SPTU.......Staff Pilot Training Unit
SQDRN...Squadron
Sqd/Ldr....Squadron Leader
TI............Target Indicator
USAF.......United States Air Force
USAAF....United States Army Air Force
VC..........Victoria Cross
VHF........Very High Frequency
W/Off......Warrant Officer
W/T.........Wireless Telegraphy
W/Cdr.....Wing Commander
WAAF......Women's Auxiliary Air Force

Book production, layout & design by Russell Holden www.PixelTweaks.co.uk
Specialising in helping self-publishers get their book into print.

Other books by John Nixon

Oh Mother, it's a Lovely Place (2009)

An illustrated history of the former RAF Millom and the station's wartime Mountain Rescue Team.

The book covers the airfield's wartime service and brief reoccupation of the station in 1953. The unit's primary purpose was the training of aircrew for Bomber Command and those airmen who passed through the station went on to have many and varied experiences of aerial warfare. From evading the Germans in occupied territory, the raid on Dresden, to the formative years of the Australian Airlines. Their stories are recounted for you here. At the heart of them all lies a small and windblown airfield which served sovereign and country through the dark days of WWII and beyond.

Wings over Sands (2012)

A history of the Cark airfield site – from the proposed airship factory development in 1916-1917 to its wartime use as RAF Cark.

Including:
No1 Staff Pilot Training Unit from 1942-1945
No 9 Light Artillery Unit
650 Squadron Anti-Aircraft Cooperation Unit
Also RAF Grange-over-Sands Equipment Officer's Training School based in the Cumbria Grand Hotel from 1941-1944.

This book will transport the reader far beyond Cumbria to such diverse locations as Iceland, South Africa, Canada, Australia, America and even Blackpool.

Reprinted in 2014 – Available on Amazon - ISBN:978-0-9927514-2-5

The Warbirds of Walney (first edition 2013)

An illustrated history of RAF Walney and 10 AGS.
SHORTLISTED IN THE 2014 LAKELAND BOOK OF THE YEAR AWARDS

Much more than simply a local history book this lavishly illustrated work will delight aviation enthusiasts, genealogists, and amateur historians alike. Providing an accessible and engaging reading experience for those seeking to understand the construction and wartime usage of this South Lakeland airfield. This limited edition of no more than 199 copies is sure to become a valuable and much sought-after resource for anyone with even a passing interest in aviation history.

"Look on the bright side chaps we could have been posted to RAF Cark!"